rather*paris*

researched, written and photographed by jon hart

toc

neighborhoods

EAT

à jean nicot
arnaud delmontel
bistrot mélac
bob's juice bar
breizh café
café de l'epoque
cafés et thés verlet
chapon chocolatier
chauvoncout
chéri bibi
coco & co
cococook
cul de poule
du pain et des idées
ets lion
glou
higuma
l'ourcine
la bague de kenza
la cabane à huîtres
la cantine de quentin
la cave à bulles
la crémerie
la pâtisserie des rèves
la pharmacie
le balzar
le baratin
le chateaubriand
le janissaire
les papilles
le train bleu
le verre volé
mamie gâteaux
marché avenue du
président wilson
marie-anne cantin
mi-va-mi
passage 53
pink flamingo pizza
pozzetto
racines
supernature

SHOP

artazart
a. simon
avenches
balouga
bda
calourette
cartes postales anciennes
chi.ind
cire trudon
comptoir des écritures
deyrolle
farida
french touche
french trotters
ie boutique
isaac reina
kitsuné
kyrie eleison
la fille du pirate
la galerie végétale
le bouclard
le jeune frères
les vélos parisiens
maison francis kurkdjian
mamie gâteaux brocante
marché aux puces de saint-
ouen
noir kennedy
objet sonore
papier+
petit pan
pigalle
pop market
serendipity
si tu veux
spree
surface to air
talc
tremblay alvergne
zut!

notes
about
paris

rather *paris* EDITOR >

Jon Hart is a jack-of-all-trades, currently trying to master relaxation. His other accomplishments include eating, drinking and shopping. Jon authored (or co-authored) eat.shop guides for Portland, San Francisco, Kansas City, Miami, NYC and, of course, Paris.

If something sounds too good to be true, I have found it usually is. I don't like being a skeptic, but I have heard too many things described as "magical" when they were simply average with a strong marketing team behind them. In a world where so many things are "spun," can anything live up to its hype? Paris does.

No matter how many times I visit Paris, my breath is always taken away while walking through the arcade of trees in the Jardin des Tuileries toward the immense and phenomenal Louvre. And not even the most flowery of culinary adjectives can make the satisfaction of consuming an authentic, fresh-from-the-oven pain aux chocolate from a top-notch boulangerie any better. There is no need to sell Paris using huckster techniques as it is, quite simply, splendid.

In my experience, the best way to experience Paris is by foot with a metro card in your pocket. When your feet can't take it anymore, get on the metro. It is super easy to figure out and will get you anywhere you want to go, fast. Weekly metro passes are worth it and are valid from Monday to Sunday. For shorter visits a *carnet* (book of ten tickets) can be purchased at a discount from automated machines. The same tickets are accepted on the clean and efficient buses, which provide one of the best and cheapest sightseeing tours on earth. I also recommend buying the little red map book "Paris Classique Par Arrondissement," it is essential to help navigate all of the tiny streets of this city and can be found at most tabacs.

In addition to the multitude of wonderful shops and restaurants in this book, here are a few other ways to spend your time in the City of Light:

1 > Act Pious: On Sunday afternoons around 4:30p, hear a free concert courtesy of a giant pipe organ while enjoying one of the most magnificent buildings in the world: Notre Dame.

2 > Act Worldly: Go to the Mosquée de Paris and experience the delights of the Arab world. One can enjoy the hammam or simply stop by for mint tea.

3 > Act Design-y: Visit Le Corbusier's Villa La Roche. Built for a collector of avant-garde art, this house is an architectural masterpiece.

4 > Act Like a Bigwig: Visit Drouot, the legendary French auction house. There is no cost to watch the auctions of incredible art and antiques; just keep your hand motions to a minimum.

it's all about...

exploring locally

*discovering a sense of place
behind the veneer of a city*

*experiencing what gives
a city its soul through its
local flavor*

rather EVOLUTION

If you are thinking this book looks suspiciously like an eat.shop guide, you're on to something. As of October 2011, the eat.shop guides evolved into **rather** to give readers a more vibrant experience when it comes to local eating and shopping. It's all about what you'd **rather** be doing with your time when you explore a city—eat at a chain restaurant or an intimate little trattoria devouring dishes the chef created from farm fresh ingredients? You get the idea.

USING **rather**

All of the businesses featured in this book are first and foremost locally owned, and they are chosen to be featured because they are authentic and uniquely conceived. And since this isn't an advertorial guide, there's no money exchanging hands • Make sure to double check the hours of the business before you go, as many places change their hours seasonally • The pictures and descriptions for each business are meant to give a feel for a place, but please know those items may no longer be available • Our maps are stylized, meaning they don't show every street • Small local businesses have always had to work that much harder to keep their heads above water, and not all the businesses featured will stay open. Please go to **rather** website for updates • **rather** editors research, shoot and write everything you see in this book • Only natural light is used to shoot and there's no styling or propping.

restaurants >
$ = inexpensive $$ = medium $$$ = expensive

Go to **rather.com** to learn more

where to lay your weary head

for more hotel choices, visit >

ParisHotel.net

PART OF THE TRAVELSHARK
TRAVEL NETWORK

hôtel amour (9th arr)
8 rue navarin
33 (0) 1 48 78 31 80
www.hotelamourparis.fr
standard double from 155 euros
notes: hotel of the moment with marc newson-
designed rooms

hôtel du petit moulin (3rd arr)
29 - 31 rue du poitou
33(0) 1 42 74 10 10
hotelpetitmoulinparis.com
standard double from 190 euros
notes: 17th century bakery turned into a stylish
christian lacroix-designed hotel

hôtel particulier montmartre (18th arr)
23 avenue junot
33 (0) 1 53 41 81 40
hotel-particulier-montmartre.com
junior double suite from 290 euros
notes: luxurious mansion with garden

hôtel saint vincent paris (7th arr)
5 rue du pré aux clercs
33 (0) 1 42 61 01 51
hotel-st-vincent.com
standard double from 290 euros
notes: delightfully serene

haven in paris
617.395.4243
haveninparis.com
studio apartments from 750 euros a week to 4
bedroom apartments from 3500 euros a week
notes: stylish rental apartments

more local gems

*these businesses appeared in
previous editions of eat.shop paris*

EAT

à la mère de famille
angora
au petit fer à cheval
bistrot paul bert
bouillon racine
bread & roses
café charbon
café de l'industrie
café vavin
chartier
chez casimir
chez prune
etablissements vinicoles
de france
granterroirs
hotel du nord
l'as du falafel
l'ecume st-honoré
l'enclos du temps
l'os à moelle
la cigale recamier
la palette
le bac a glaces
le bistrot du peintre
le c'amelot
le nemrod
le petit lutetia
le petit vatel
le progrès
le pure café
le rubis
le taxi jaune
le timbre
les cakes de bertrand
marché boulevard raspail
marie quatrehomme
pâtisserie sadaharu aoki
pho banh cuon 14
rose bakery
saint germain crêperie
tesnime
tokyo eat

SHOP

atypyk
biscuit sec
blackblock
carouche
celis
chône
coquelicot paprika
cuisinophile
dominique picquier
e. dehillerin
emmanuelle zysman
erotokritos
et puis c'est tout!
58m
gaspard yurkievich
hoses
jouets
bass
l'objet
l'objet qui parle
la droguerie
lieu commun
liwan
liza korn
m.a. dauliac
magasin sennelier
marché saint-pierre
marie papier
miller et bertaux
ofr
pages 50/70
patyka
porte de vanve flea market
renhsen
shine
the collection
the lazy dog
tsumori chisato
ultramod
voyages

notes

1st / 2nd arr.

louvre, palais royal

eat

shop

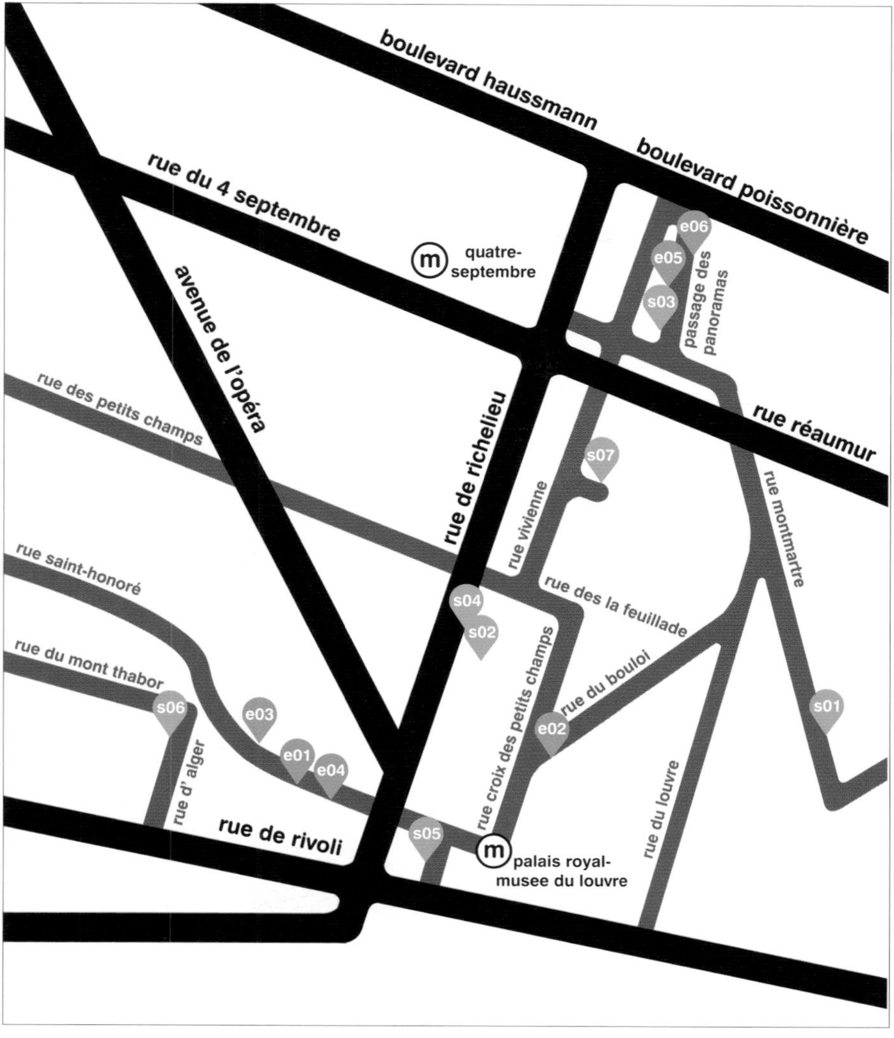
boulevard haussmann
boulevard poissonnière
rue du 4 septembre
quatre-
septembre
avenue de l'opéra
rue de richelieu
passage des
panoramas
rue réaumur
rue des petits champs
rue vivienne
rue montmartre
rue saint-honoré
rue des la feuillade
rue croix des petits champs
rue du bouloi
rue du mont thabor
rue d' alger
rue du louvre
rue de rivoli
palais royal-
musee du louvre
e01
e02
e03
e04
e05
e06
s01
s02
s03
s04
s05
s06
s07

a. simon

hotel and restaurant supplies

48 - 52 Rue Montmartre
Corner of Rue Etienne Marcel
(2nd Arr) *map S01*
Metro 4: Les Halles
33 (0) 1 42 33 71 65

mon 1:30 - 6:30p tue - fri 9a - 6:30p
sat 9:30a - 6:30p

Yes, Please: *gite à paté oval dish, enameled round address numbers, sausage stuffer, crêpe iron cleaning brush, frites cutter, printed linen dish towels, chef coats*

Of all the common fantasies of fleeing one's humdrum life, moving to Paris and opening a charming little café has got to be one of the most desirable. Pouring glasses of Ricard for handsome *madames* and *monsieurs* sounds infinitely more appealing than analyzing forecast charts in Des Moines, doesn't it? Well dear, disgruntled workers, A. Simon is the first step to your new exciting life. At this Parisian institution, you will find all the necessary equipment to open said fantasy café or bistro. There is nothing really stopping you now, as A. Simon is open six days a week. Hop to it.

à jean nicot

in search of a delicious croque monsieur

173 Rue Saint-Honoré
Between Rue des Pyramides and
Rue de l'Echelle (1st Arr) *map E01*
Metro 1: Palais Royal - Musée du Louvre
33 (0) 1 42 60 49 77

mon - fri 7:30a - 9p
sat - sun 9a - 8p
lunch. dinner. coffee / tea. snacks
$ first come, first served

Yes, Please: *pelforth blonde, ricard, café créme, niçoise au thon, croque monsieur, croque saint-honoré, tartine savoyarde, assiette du fromage*

I have searched high and low in this backwater food town for a brasserie that creates a gastronomically superior, fabulously gooey croque monsieur. Sadly the best croque I have ever eaten was in Seattle. For shame, Paris. This is like saying the best grilled cheese you ever ate was in Tibet. But then I visited a particularly photogenic tabac called À Jean Nicot. Finally—a hot, melty triad of meat, bread and cheese that measured up to my fantasies of what a real croque monsieur should be! No need to gild the lily here, except for maybe a little mustard on the side.

avenches

singularly artistic jewelry

43 Galerie Montpensier
In the Jardin du Palais Royal
(1st Arr) *map S02*
Metro 1: Palais Royal - Musée du Louvre
33 (0) 1 42 74 04 28
www.avenches-paris.com

tue - sat noon - 7p
custom orders / design

Yes, Please: *coiled chain & precious stone*
necklaces, coiled silver wire & stone bracelets,
coiled wire rings, gold lip brooch

Over the years I have worked on these guides, I have come across a few artisans whose work has so impressed me, I felt like a talent agent seeing the young Meryl Streep in an early performance. Jewelry maker Vincent Vaucher is such a find. His miniscule Marais shop, **Avenches**, is a singular vision of an artist whose aesthetic straddles vulnerability and elegance. His pieces are made with exquisite craftsmanship and luxurious yet understated materials. I had to restrain my wanton enthusiasm so as not to destroy the perfect, serene mood here. He is one to watch.

café de l'epoque

a classic brasserie

2 Rue du Bouloi
Corner of Rue Croix des Petits Champs
(1st Arr) *map E02*
Metro 1: Palais Royal - Musée du Louvre
33 (0) 1 42 33 40 70

mon - sun 11:30a - 11p
lunch. dinner. full bar
$-$$ reservations accepted

Yes, Please: *coca light, poireaux vinaigrette,*
assiette de sauton foie & toasts, saucisson de lyon
& salade lentilles, tartare de boeuf, profiterole chocolat

You won't be without options for a place to rest your weary feet in Paris, so how to choose? Follow my hints to eliminate the not-so-good options. If most of the patrons are reading Rick Steves guides, keep walking. A roving accordionist hovers. Run! The menu indicates all food is on sale. Dud! If you are near the Palais Royal, go to one of my fave classics: **Café de l'Epoque**. Not only does it pass all of my tests, but it also offers very good, straight-ahead food and drink. And it's mere yards from the Louboutin shop, handy for catching your breath after dropping 1,000 clams for some new heels.

cafés et thés verlet

coffee beans and drinks

256 Rue Saint-Honoré
Between Rue Saint-Anne and
Rue des Pyramides (1st Arr) *map E03*
Metro 1: Palais Royal - Musée du Louvre
33 (0) 1 42 60 67 39
www.cafesverlet.com

mon - sat 9a - 7p
coffee / tea. treats
$ first come, first served

Yes. Please: *coffees: australia skybury, guatemala antigua victory; teas: keemun f. o. p., golden tips, mokalbari; vanille noisette*

Let's get one thing straight. Everything is not better in France. In fact, this country has a dirty little secret. The coffee is not that good unless you like it espresso-like (i.e., extremely dark), kind of burnt tasting, and always requiring sugar. But fear not, as there's **Cafés et Thés Verlet**. This historic café is a rare gem in Paris. Not only are the exotic coffee beans and teas that are sold in bulk here chosen for subtlety and complexity, this is also where to get a cup of really good coffee. Though I may sound rigid and pigheaded, like I require my morning frappuccino—*au contraire*, a venti mocha works for me too.

cartes postales anciennes

antique postcards from exotic places

50 Passage des Panoramas
Between Boulevard Poissonnière and
Rue Saint-Marc (2nd Arr) *map S03*
Metro 8/9: Grands Boulevards
33 (0) 1 42 33 49 95

mon - sat 10a - 6:30p

Yes, Please: *a sampling of postcard categories:
afrique du sud, moroc, italie, napoleon, la seine,
the sea, oddities*

These days, everything is in transition, and many things we once thought were rock solid are just hollow facades (Bernie Madoff, Tiger Woods). Not to get too serious, but the times have me reflecting. This might be why I became transfixed at the antique postcard shops in the Passage Panorama. My favorite is **Cartes Postales Anciennes**. No beach babes holding brewskies on cards here, but rather cards sent long ago from travels to Turkey, Iran, India—when the written word was revered. The glimpse back at this pre-digital era feels poignant, like a hint at forgotten wisdom, or a much-needed escape from reality.

higuma
restorative japanese fare

163 Rue Saint-Honoré
Corner of Avenue de l'Opera
(1st Arr) *map E04*
Metro 1: Palais Royal - Musée du Louvre
See website for other location
33 (0) 1 58 62 49 22
www.higuma.fr

mon - sun 11:30a - 10:30p
lunch. dinner
$-$$ first come, first served

Yes. Please: *heineken, jasmine tea, shoyu ramen, miso ramen, killer gyoza, yakinikudon, kimchi ramen, butter corn ramen*

Yes, I love French food. Rich, meaty *plats* are divine—but too much offal can really throw your system for a loop. The antidote to this is bright, clean flavors and satisfying, nurturing dishes. In Paris, I get this respite at **Higuma**. One plate of gyoza can counter all of those livers and gizzards and get me back to neutral, fast. I think of this place as a reset button transporting me back to my factory default settings. Obviously I'm not the only one who feels this way, as **Higuma** has a new second location. Keep this address in your back pocket and you won't need that roll of Tums.

kitsuné

art, music and fashion all-in-one

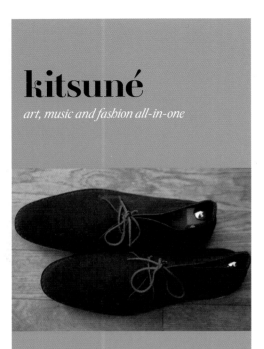

52 Rue de Richelieu
Corner of Rue des Petits Champs
(1st Arr) *map S04*
Metro 1: Palais Royal - Musée du Louvre
33 (0) 1 42 60 34 28
www.kitsune.fr

twitter @maisonkitsune
tue - sat 11a - 7:30p

Yes, Please: *kitsuné: white button shirt with black piping, navy-inspired cable knit sweater, red, white & blue western-inspired shirt, pierre hardy collaboration shoes*

AU
PAIN
D'ÉPICES

One of the reasons I didn't become a fashion designer is my addiction to sweatpants. You see, one has to be 100% committed to fashion to have one's designs taken seriously, and I cannot live without my elastic-waisted fuzzy pants. This is not to say I don't love wearing nice clothes, though. I'd wear about anything from **Kitsuné**, a Paris-based design house headed by a stylish designer/dj duo. Silhouettes are part preppy, part Japanese arty—these clothes are as cool as their originators. I think of **Kitsuné** as the warm-up wear to my cozy pants.

la fille du pirate

nautical antiques and miniatures

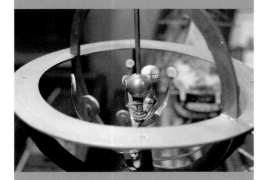

2 Place du Palais Royal
Corner of Rue Valois (1st Arr) *map S05*
Metro 1: Palais Royal - Musée du Louvre
33 (0) 1 42 60 20 30
www.lafilledupirate.com

tue - sun 11a - 7p

Yes, Please: *incredible replicas of sailing ships, sextants, scrimshawed whalebone, antique globes, looking glasses, porthole windows, nautical-themed oil paintings*

I felt like I'd discovered the land of miniature people, Lilliput, entering La Fille du Pirate. This amazing shop, near the Louvre, offers all things nautical but specializes in miniature antique replicas of seagoing vessels. These museum-quality models are incredible. The impeccable craftsmanship scales all the way down to miniature-sized ropes operating wee-sized sails, as if they were actual full-sized ships. I asked the shopkeeper if he would tie me up, so I could pretend to be Gulliver awaking in Lilliput. Perhaps I used the wrong French words for tie me up, as he politely declined and asked me to leave.

maison francis kurkdjian

paris perfumerie

5 Rue d'Alger
Between Rue de Rivoli and
Rue du Mont Thabor (1st Arr) *map S06*
Metro 1: Tuileries
33 (0) 42 60 07 07
www.franciskurkdjian.com

twitter @fkurkdjian
mon - fri 11a - 1:30p, 2:30 - 7p
sat 11a - 7p
online shopping. custom scents

Yes, Please: *eau de parfum: lumière noire, apom, aqua universalis; papiers encens, le bracelet parfumé, les bulles d'agathe cut herbs, parfums d'intérieur*

Remember back when you would buy a perfume in Paris because it was a unique souvenir? This is an old-fashioned notion, because fragrances have become ubiquitous, duty-free schlock. **Maison Francis Kurkdjian** revives the conviction that a French perfume is a distinct and romantic embodiment of this city. Francis has made scents for many of the big French couture houses. Now, under his own name, he offers fragrances in both day and evening varieties, and you can even have a signature scent made by appointment. Save your duty-free dollars for giant Toblerone bars.

passage 53

gloriously nuanced cuisine

53 Passage des Panoramas
Between Boulevard Poissonnière and
Rue Saint-Marc (2nd Arr) *map E05*
Metro 8/9: Grands Boulevards
33 (0) 1 42 33 04 35
www.passage53.com

tue – sat 12:30 – 2:30p, 8p – close
lunch. dinner
$$$ reservations recommended

Yes, Please: *jacquesson champagne; degustation menu: pumpkin with coffee foam, veal tartare with raw oyster, calamari on almond & cauliflower cream*

Even though I eat for a living, the number of lunches I've spent over $100 on is small. At dinner I'll open the wallet, but my Midwest upbringing makes it hard for me to give it up at lunch. At **Passage 53**, I had a change of heart. This beautifully spare place located in the beautifully ornate Passage des Panoramas is a celebration of subtlety. With nuance and virtuosity, chef Sato sent out the courses (either five or eight). Prepared like minimalist assemblages, these dishes command you to delight in their delicate perfection and flawless balance. One bite and I realized I was eating small masterpieces. I would have paid any price.

racines

simple and stellar food, natural wines

8 Passage des Panoramas
Between Boulevard Poissonnière and
Rue Saint-Marc (2nd Arr) *map E06*
Metro 8/9: Grands Boulevards
33 (0) 1 40 13 06 41
www.morethanorganic.com

mon - fri 12:30 - 2:30p, 8p - midnight
lunch. dinner. wine
$$-$$$ reservations recommended

Á TABLE...

LES ENTRÉES:
LA PLANCHE DE LARD DE COLONNATA...
SALADE DE TÊTE DE COCHON AUX POMMES DE TERRE
ST-JACQUES DE BRETAGNE AU LARD DE COLONNATA...
FOIE GRAS "EXTRA" AUX POMMES...

LES PLATS:
COCHON DE LAIT "NOIR DE BIGORRE", RUTABAGA AU LARD...
CANARD DE CHALLANS SUR LA PEAU...
POULARDE "RACINES", P'TITS LÉGUMES...
DOS DE BAR DE LIGNE, POIREAUX À L'HUILE DE SÉSAME...

LE FROMAGE > DESSERT:
CONTÉ "2OT" DE MARCEL PETITE...
TARTE AU CHOCOLAT NOIR > CAROUBE...

Yes, Please: *06 emmanuel bouillon arbois pupillin, saint jacques de bretagne au lard, foie gras "extra" aux pommes, cochon de lait "noir de bigorre" rutabaga au lard*

Upon tasting the braised pork and root vegetables at Racines, I was smitten. I find this to be one of the most satisfying food combos: robust proteins with a delectable side. It feels like masculine food, but prepared with a delicate touch. I finished the food and a bottle of gorgeous riesling and left with a serious man-crush. In subsequent days I would try many other restaurants, never able to shake the memory of the perfectly seared scallops served under a silken blanket of lardo that I had adored here. Eating at other places felt like cheating on my true love. **Racines**, you had me at hello.

si tu veux

good old-fashioned toy shop

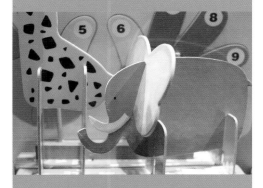

68 Galerie Vivienne
Near Rue Vivienne (2nd Arr) *map S07*
Metro 3: Bourse
33 (0) 1 42 60 59 97
www.situveuxjouer.com

twitter @situveuxjouer
mon - sat 10:30a - 7p

Yes, Please: *paper swords, rope ring toss, marble run, goki football game, chateau building blocks, crazy campers game, "c'est moi le plus beau" book*

It is impossible for me to fathom being raised in Paris. It's got to be so different from the way I was raised in the middle of America. For example, the idea of being a kid and getting to choose a holiday gift at **Si Tu Veux** is enthralling compared to my own experience going to Christmasland at the local Farm and Fleet. The game I used to plead for, Hungry Hungry Hippos, pales in comparison to the build-your-own chateaux kit I saw here. Who knows? Maybe you get blasé about chateaus when you are around them all of the time, but it would be fun to be a kid again, living in Paris to find out.

3rd / 4th arr.

le marais

eat

shop

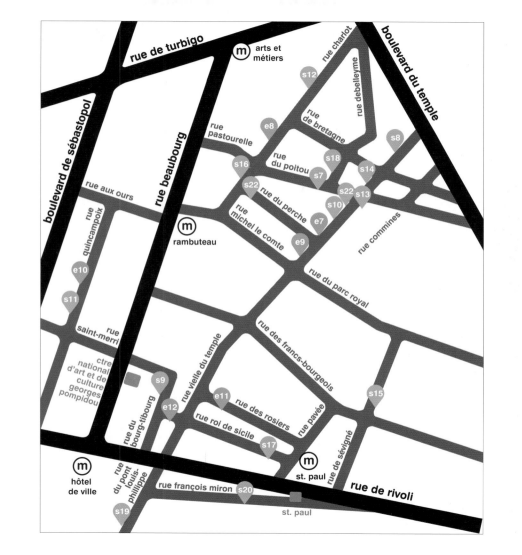

balouga
modern furniture for children

25 Rue des Filles du Calvaire
Between Boulevard du Temple and
Rue de Turenne (3rd Arr) *map S08*
Metro 8: Filles du Calvaire
33 (0) 1 42 74 01 49
www.balouga.com

tue - fri 12:30 - 7p sat 2 - 7p
online shopping

Yes, Please: *balouga edition furniture, miller goodman shape maker, string swedish shelving, lunatic desk system, meridiana cuckoo clock, kazam desk*

Sophisticated parents often try to influence their kids to make elevated choices. This only leads to disappointment when the little cherub chooses a Bratz doll and names it "Sweet Princess of the Pinkland Dreams." The moral here: let your offspring figure some stuff out on their own. However, parents can make decisions that will leave a lasting impression. Furnishing his/her room with wee-sized design classics from **Balouga** is a primer to the world of good design. Kids may not realize they are being influenced, but they will be happy down the road when they have outgrown fairyland chic.

breizh café

breton crêperie

109 Rue Vieille du Temple
Corner of Rue du Perche (3rd Arr) *map E07*
Metro 8: Saint-Sébastien Froissart
33 (0) 1 42 72 13 77
www.breizhcafe.com

wed - sun noon - 11p
lunch. dinner
$-$$ first come, first served

Yes. Please: *thé vert, chocolat chaud "maison;" crêpes:*
beurre, yuzu & sucre, dame tatin, campagnarde, paysanne;
cancale oysters

I know, I know. A crêpe shop in Paris, whodathunkit? Well keep your sardonic criticisms to yourself until you try **Breizh Café**. This is not your normal street vendor selling fluffernutter roll-ups. I'm talking farm-fresh eggs, homemade caramel, fresh butter from Breton, unpasteurized Gruyère. Everything is made fresh from the best ingredients available and served in an extremely pleasant, modern environment. Still haven't convinced you? Dozens of artisanal ciders should be enough to win over even the most jaded of grumps. I know you are sold now. And if you aren't, fine. More for the rest of us.

calourette

tempting accessories

27 Rue du Bourg-Tibourg
Between Rue de la Verrerie and Rue Sainte-
Croix de la Bretonnerie (4th Arr) *map S09*
Metro 1/11: Hôtel de Ville
33 (0) 1 48 04 08 25
www.calourette.com

tue - sun 2 - 7:30p
online shopping

Yes, Please: *calourette jewelry, schmoove, bernstock speirs hats, agnelle gloves, tricolore tee's, babbu scarves, spring court shoes, camo sweaters*

Some people are pulled together; others not. I don't think I am, but I am beginning to understand how to do it. What I mean is that certain people can throw on jeans and a t-shirt, clean or dirty, add a necklace, and they look amazing. So I've figured out that a necklace, or a hat, or a scarf, mixed with a cup of self-confidence makes it all work. **Calourette** would be a good place to start adding accessories esteem. This shop is filled with fun extras made by Marianne Rautureau or sourced by her. She's got "it," and with a few more adornments, I hope to have "it," too.

ch. ind

paris designer of sassy tops for women

117 Rue Vieille du Temple
Between Rue du Perche and
Rue Debelleyme (3rd Arr) *map S10*
Metro 8: Filles du Calvaire
33 (0) 1 42 74 05 70

tue - sat 11a - 2p, 3 - 7:30p
sun - mon 2 - 7:30p

Yes. Please: *ch. ind shirts: grace, geny, coco striped &*
ruffled, douard men's style; luce jumpsuit, fred cashmere
sweater, gaby overcoat

Plopping down in a city for a long period is great fun. You really get to know a place when stationed there for weeks, or months! I have discovered a downside however. Not unlike a runner hitting "the wall," I sometimes will wake up and think, I can't bear to wear this ratty old sweater one more day. If I were a girl having that type of day, I'd go to **ch. ind**. Designed and sewn in-house, the sassy tops here are fun, beautifully made and reasonably priced. Replicas of men's oxford shirts with a young, sexy-girl silhouette could become such a fave, you might ditch your old duds altogether.

cococook

delicious food to go

3 Rue Charlot
Between Rue Pastourelle and
Rue de Bretagne (3rd Arr) *map E08*
Metro 8: Filles du Calvaire
33 (0) 1 42 74 80 00
www.cococook.com

mon - sun 11:30a - 10:30p
lunch. dinner
$-$$ first come, first served

Yes, Please: *06 les grimaudes, jus rouge, salade carottes aux herbes, sandwich cococlub, soupe de petits pois & aman-des, poulet fermier au quinoa, cake chocolat & courgette*

Sure, eating out in Paris is fantastic, but there are rules and confines. Eight pm is the earliest seating, and if you don't have a reservation, it's panic time. Thankfully, eating *in* in Paris can be pretty great also, especially when it involves good food, good wine and good friends. But you need to know where to get the take-out. No need to have panic time—**Cococook** is an excellent option. It's like visiting your chef friend's refrigerator; the foods here are healthy and scrumptious. And those who prefer sleep over nightlife can have friends over to eat and still be in bed by 11. Perfect.

comptoir des écritures

beautiful equipment for writing

35 Rue Quincampoix
Between Rue Berger and
Rue Rambuteau (4th Arr) *map S11*
Metro 3: Rambuteau
33 (0) 1 42 78 95 10
www.comptoirdesecritures.com

twitter @comptoirdes
tue - fri 11a - 7p sat 11a - 6p
online shopping

Yes, Please: *le papier by lucien polastron, raw pigments, handmade writing paper, quills, calligraphy postcards, handmade books, zeichentusche inks, calligraphy brushes*

I have a befuddling disconnect in accordance to expensive things. I'm the opposite of a crow—I will stop to pick up a piece of twine while ignoring a five-carat diamond next to it. This is why **Comptoir des Écritures,** a shop selling Asian inks and papers for calligraphers, makes me melt into a puddle of goo. Stacks of oatmeal-colored handmade paper—perfectly proportioned and precisely stacked on a golden wooden tray—are far better than the Hope Diamond in my mind. Everything here is so considered and beautiful, yet made of such common materials. This is like heaven for us non-crows.

farida

men's and women's self-assured fashions

61 Rue Charlot
Corner of Rue du Forez (3rd Arr) *map S12*
Metro 8: Filles du Calvaire
33 (0) 1 42 78 71 09

tue - sat 11a - 8p
sun 2 - 7p

Yes, Please: *vivienne westwood, opening ceremony, heal, carven, 0044, david szeto, jas mb, eley kishimoto*

If the fashion continuum ranges from 1 (Jil Sander white shirts) to 10 (Lacroix couture), my wardrobe is filled with 3s. Wearing boring button-downs and chinos with the occasional sport coat thrown on should disqualify me from doing this job. Even though I am a 3 dresser, nothing makes me happier than the numbers over 5. Farida, a former stylist, has an eye for clothing and accessories with panache. With a large selection of Vivienne Westwood, **Farida** (the store) features fashion at its most creative, with clothing that show outrageous can also be tasteful. Memo to self: incorporate more animal prints into my wardrobe.

french trotters

clothing for men

116 Rue Vieille du Temple
Corner of Rue Debelleyme
(3rd Arr) *map S13*
Metro 8: Saint Sébastien Froissart
See website for other locations
33 (0) 1 44 61 00 14
www.frenchtrotters.fr

twitter @frenchtrotters
tue - sat 11a - 7:30p
sun - mon 2:30 - 7:30p

Yes, Please: *vintage casio watches, mismo bags, commune de paris, b store, volta, libertine - libertine, gitman brothers ties, opening ceremony*

I met the French Trotters duo Clarent and Carole while working on the first edition of eat.shop. At the time, I had to stifle my *Talented Mr. Ripley* urges, fantasizing how I could take over their enviable life of travel. A rare moment of good judgment kept me from pursuing this desire, allowing the duo to prosper, opening a new menswear shop. Their discriminating taste and restrained style once again garnered critical acclaim. As I checked out the offerings at this new store, I felt the familiar jealousy return, and I found myself muttering under my breath, *"Je m'appelle Clarent."*

glou

a food insider's take on cozy dining

101 Rue Vieille du Temple
Between Rue des Quatre Fils and
Rue du Perche (3rd Arr) *map E09*
Metro 8: Saint-Sébastien Froissart
33 (0) 1 42 74 44 32
www.glou-resto.com

mon - sun noon - 2:30p, 8 - 11p
lunch. dinner
\$\$ reservations recommended

Yes, Please: *07 pierre gaillard rhône, lardo di colonnata de fausto guadagni, palette ibérico bellota, echine de cochon basque roquefort vieux berger*

With the closing of many of America's beloved magazines comes lots of unemployed, creative people with time on their hands. I say that when a setback comes, it's an opportunity to do something you've always wanted. Julien is an example of this. After his stint as the editor of France's premier food magazine *Régal* ended, he opened **Glou**. This warm and inviting bistro has a super wine selection and specializes in simple fare made exceptionally well. I say **Glou** is the culmination of years of writing about food. Ruth Reichl, are you listening?

ie boutique

everyday objects and kids' clothing from india

128 Rue Vieille du Temple
Between Rue de Turenne and
Rue Pastourelle (3rd Arr) *map S14*
Metro 8: Filles du Calvaire
33 (0) 1 44 59 87 72

tue - sun 11a - 8p

Yes, Please: *indian cut out figures, antique bells, colorful printed cotton yardage, clothing for kids made from imported cotton, indian barbie, colorful slippers*

One of my great joys when it comes to travelling is bringing home mundane, everyday objects from the countries I visit. For example: my beloved French stapler—every time I use it, I smile, thinking about my fantastic trip. The wares at **IE Boutique** are all everyday objects that one would find in India, and though they are ubiquitous in that part of the world, they are worlds away from being mundane. There's everything from buttons to Indian Barbie—which is far more exotic and cool than, say, Palm Beach Swim Suit Barbie.

isaac reina

leather goods for men and women

38 Rue de Sévigné
Between Rue du Parc Royal and Rue des
Francs Bourgeois (3rd Arr) *map S15*
Metro 8: Chemin Vert
33 (0) 1 42 78 81 95
www.isaacreina.com

tue - sat 11a - 7:30p

Yes, Please: *isaac reina: magic box necessaire, 014 sac 48h standard, 043 sac 24h, 144 for make up soft pouch, 148 magic trotter bag, 161 porte documents "classify"*

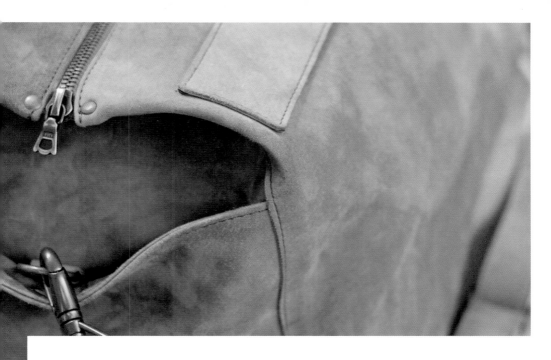

A minimalist painter friend of mine drives me crazy, spending days deciding where to make the faintest mark to finish a work. I want to scream, "Loosen up." But in looking at **Isaac Reina**'s exquisite leather bags and accessories, it's clear to me that spending the time to get your work exactly right pays off. Having designed accessories for Hermès and M. Margiela, Mr. Reina has a golden provenance, and his buttery leathers are perfect: in proportion, in craftsmanship, in their utilitarian elegance. Isaac's leather pieces prove that minimalism can be masterful.

la cave à bulles

french artisanal beer store

45 Rue Quincampoix
Between Rue Berger and
Rue Rambuteau (4th Arr) *map E10*
Metro 11: Rambuteau
33 (0) 1 40 29 03 69
www.caveabulles.fr

tue - sat 10a - 2p, 4 - 8p
$-$$ first come, first served

Yes, Please: *beers: thomas becket bière de bourgogne,
northern blanche, juliette-brasserie uberach, la chardon
rouge, la bière des collines, ninkasi triple, la clandestine*

In wine-loving France, beer is like the earthworm of the alcohol world. It is underappreciated, undervalued and hard to find. That is until **La Cave à Bulles** opened. Owner Simon, who is quite charismatic and not worm-like at all, is spreading the word about beers of this country. I am not kidding when I divulge, though I have been traveling to Paris for well over a decade, I have neither heard of nor tasted 90% of the beers available here. Simon realizes there's lots of work to do, which is why he offers classes to small groups to educate about *les beers*. Here's mud in your eye!

le bouclard

avant fashion

15 Rue Charlot
Corner of Rue Pastourelle
(3rd Arr) *map S16*
Metro 8: Filles du Calvaire
33 (0) 1 42 36 14 66
www.le-bouclard.com

tue - sat 1 - 7p
online shopping

Yes. Please: *le bouclard brand, final home, vans by volt, sns herning, rick owens for eastpak, tsumori chisato, cabane de zucca, artysm*

Paris can be intimidating. Between the historicalness of it all and the chicness everywhere you look, it's easy to feel like the country mouse. At **Le Bouclard,** my hick-o-meter flared. Feeling nervous, I picked up a gorgeous shoe, acting like I was thinking of trying it on. Owner Cecile Audouin said, "I don't think that will fit you—it's for a woman." I laughed. She laughed. At that moment I knew that there was no reason to be intimidated. Though she's a Parisienne and I'm an Oregonian, we both shared the same interest—an appreciation of beautiful things.

mi-va-mi

some of the best falafels in paris

23 Rue des Rosiers
Near Rue des Ecouffes (4th Arr) *map E11*
Metro 4: Saint Paul
33 (0) 42 71 53 72

mon - thu 11a - midnight fri 11a - 7p
sun 11a - midnight
lunch. dinner. wine / beer
$ first come, first served

Yes, Please: *jus naturel, heineken, pita falafel,*
pita shawarma, brochette dinde, assiette keftas,
assiette de frites, pita merguez

Where I live, there's something called "The Oregon Vortex." Though bumper stickers are offered up as proof, I'm a skeptic. I can, however, prove there is a Paris vortex. A corner in the Marais is home to not one, but two of the best falafel shops in the world: **L' as du Falafel** (featured in the first edition of *eat.shop paris*) and **Mi-Va-Mi** directly across the street. It's totally different in style from its competitor but just as good (maybe better). The only thing to do is try them both and decide for yourself. And don't forget to buy your "Paris Vortex" bumper sticker, checks payable to: Jon's Awesome Business.

noir
kennedy

youthful rocker style

12 and 22 Rue du Roi de Sicile
Corner of Rue Pavée (4th Arr) *map S17*
Metro 1: Saint Paul
33 (0) 1 42 71 15 50
www.noirkennedy.fr

mon 1 - 8p tue - sat 11a - 8p
sun 2 - 8p

Yes. Please: *noir kennedy printed tees & jeans, vintage vans, vintage americana clothing, vintage wing tips, french foreign legion jackets, cheap monday, bowler hats*

One of my all-time, top-five ways to let loose is driving in the car alone, singing at top volume to my favorite music. This is my way of living out a fantasy persona that has me as the lead singer of Bauhaus. I feel a bit wimpy that I've never come out of my goth rock closet. Maybe if I were younger I would and I'd shop at **Noir Kennedy**. I'd find everything here for my secret fantasy life from super-tight skinny jeans to vintage wingtips. The style here is a touch rockabilly mixed with goth. On the whole, it's all about rocker attitude. Just like me when I'm driving in my Volkswagen.

objet sonore

incredible vintage stereo equipment

19 Rue Debelleyme
Between Rue du Poitou and
Rue de Bretagne (3rd Arr) *map S18*
Metro 8: Filles du Calvaire
33 (0) 9 50 48 34 18
www.presence-audio.com

tue - sat 10:30a - 7:30p
online shopping

Yes, Please: *vintage stereo equipment:*
marantz, braun, technics, thorens, bang & olufsen,
grundig, brionvega

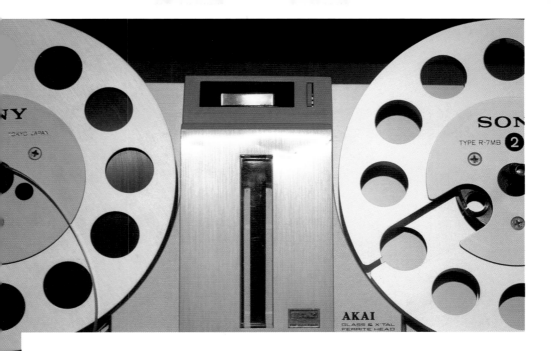

I am willing to be a total nerd when it comes to certain things. Vintage stereo equipment makes me wave my geek flag high. The combination of superior technology and stellar '60s and '70s design is a total bull's-eye into awesometown. I'd fill every room in my house with one of these masterpieces if I won the lottery, and then I'd buy two more houses and fill them up. I'd say **Objet Sonore** is almost too good to be true. Vintage Braun designs by Dieter Rams next to pristine Bang & Olufsen turntables—I feel my heart palpitating.

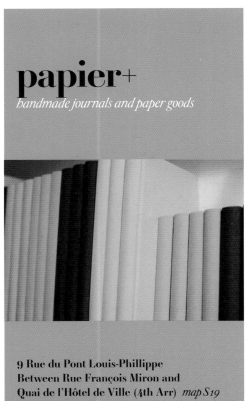

papier+

handmade journals and paper goods

9 Rue du Pont Louis-Phillippe
Between Rue François Miron and
Quai de l'Hôtel de Ville (4th Arr) *map S19*
Metro 1: Saint Paul
33 (0) 1 42 77 70 49
www.papierplus.com

mon - sat noon - 7p
online shopping

Yes, Please: *presentation boxes, artist's portfolios, binders, colored stationery, photo albums with window, press books, autograph books, journals*

One to follow tradition, I looked up a list of gifts I should give on certain occasions. I found that the first wedding anniversary is about giving paper. My first thought was what a disappointment to get the good stuff in the first year. Who cares about silver, which requires 25 years of matrimony? Obviously I love fine paper and stationery. This is why **Papier+** resonates with me so. I look at the beautiful binders and journals, carefully crafted, and I am moved by the potential creativity. And when I see the careful placement given to a stack of fine writing paper, I realize I'm not the only one who cares about paper.

petit pan

magical children's decor and furnishings

39 Rue François Miron
Between Rue de Fourcy and Rue Tiron
Metro 1: Saint Paul
(4th Arr) *map S20*
33 (0) 1 42 74 57 16
www.petitpan.com

tue - sat 10:30a - 2p, 3 - 7:30p

Yes, Please: *silk duck kites, bamboo & silk lanterns, guirlande étoiles, mushroom mobiles, garland fêtes, brio toys, kid quilts, gouache*

Petit Pan thrust me into the children's world of make believe. Full-size busts of polar bears and larger than life butterflies meticulously handmade of painted silk and bamboo illuminate the walls and ceilings like a friendly, cartoon-like episode of *Wild Kingdom.* I swear I could hear the sound of banjos playing "The Country Bear Jamboree" as I entered the animated vignette of a campfire complete with water boiling in a cooking pot. I felt like I was taking a mini safari into the owner's imagination, with thankfully no worries about a stampede.

pozzetto

silky gelato majesty

39 Rue du Roi de Sicile
Between Rue Vieille du Temple and
Rue du Bourg-Tibourg (4th Arr) *map E12*
Metro 1: Saint Paul
33 (0) 1 42 77 08 64
www.pozzetto.biz

twitter @pozzettoparis
mon - thu 10a - 10:30p
fri - sat 10a - midnight sun 10a - 11p
treats. coffee / tea
$ first come, first served

Yes, Please: *caffè con panna; gelato: gianduja torinese, pistacchio di sicilia, nocciola piemonte, fior di latte, cioccolato fondente, yogurt magro, zabaione*

Normally I quiver with excitement to eat Pozzetto's gelato. It's the perfect respite after a long day of shopping in the Marais. However, on the day I was last there, in the middle of November, the temperature was near freezing and a concoction of frozen eggs and cream wasn't too appealing. Still, I was on the clock, so I ordered from the bored employee. I took a few pictures then sat on a nearby bench and continued to do my job—eating the gelato. As it started to sleet, a man approached and said, "Where do I find such a magnificent treat?" I pointed to **Pozzetto** and happily got back to work.

surface
to air

hip, young clothing and accessories

**108 Rue Vieille du Temple
Corner of Rue Debelleyme
(3rd Arr)** *map S21*
**Metro 8: Filles du Calvaire
33 (0) 1 44 61 76 27
www.surfacetoair.com**

twitter @surfacetoair
mon - sat 11:30a - 7:30p
sun 1:30 - 7:30p
online shopping

Yes, Please: *surface to air: trap jaw pendant, three finger rings, dotty skirt, men's shawl cardigan, claude classic shirt, edward lace boots, buckle ankle boot*

When in Paris, I love it when I appear so "with it" that someone will ask me for directions. One day a couple of American hipsters asked me where to find The Surface of Air. I rolled my eyes that they mangled the name of this Parisian art, design and fashion institution. I mustered a fake French accent and sent them off to Rue Charlot. I was feeling quite proud of myself until later that day when I went to **Surface to Air** to take pictures for this book, only to find it gone. It had recently moved into a new flagship shop on a different street. So much for Mr. Know-It-All.

tremblay
alvergne

preppy yet hip men's clothing

11 Rue du Perche
Between Rue Charlot and
Rue Vieille du Temple (3rd Arr) *map S22*
Metro 8: Filles du Calvaire
33 (0) 1 42 74 15 35
www.tremblay-alvergne.com

tue - sat 11:30a - 7:30p
sun 2 - 7p

Yes. Please: *tremblay alvergne: harris tweed jacket, jersey cotton shirts, wool, cotton & cashmere cardigan, corduroy button-down shirt*

It is easy to fantasize about what life could be like but never make the changes. I've certainly said, "Oh, I'll do that when I'm older." Call me Tony Robbins, but today is the first day of the rest of my life! And I am going to wear nicer clothes. First stop: **Tremblay Alvergne**. This Paris-based designer creates clothes that would make the strictest of lifestyle coaches take notice. Made of wool and cashmere, knit tops and blazers are tailored—a bit preppy but hip, and not at all country club. With my new look pulled together, I'm ready to start my inspirational lecture series soon at a Holiday Inn near you.

5th arr.

le quartier latin

eat

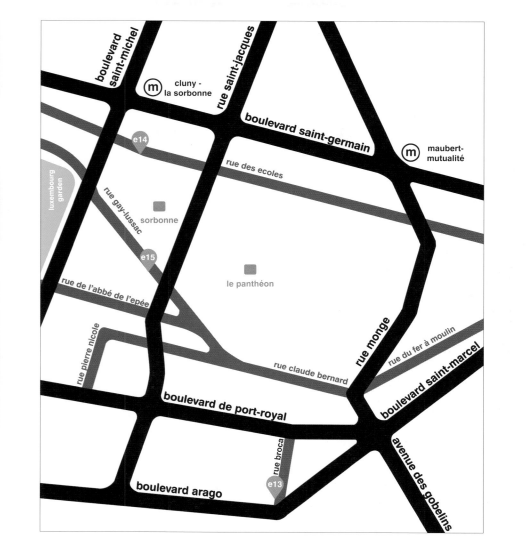

l'ourcine

chef driven bistro

92 Rue Broca
Between Boulevard Arago and Boulevard
de Port-Royal (13th Arr) *map E13*
Metro 6: Denfert Rochereau
33 (0) 1 47 07 13 65

tue - sat noon – 2:30p, 7 - 10:30p
lunch, dinner
$$ reservations recommended

Yes, Please: *consommé de sauvageon juste crème,
croutons & ciboulette, filet mignon de porc rôti à l'ail confit,
dos de sanglier cuisiné au beurre persillé*

Paris' magnificent buildings and rich cultural history make it the most touristed city on earth. Think of it as Euro Disney for grown-ups. Since it is a tourist mecca—there are numerous traps, especially when it comes to dining—real gems can be hard to find. **L'Ourcine** is located on a street you would never just happen down, yet you should definitely find. Opened by celebrated chef Sylvain Danière, **L'Ourcine** presents his marvelous take on the classics. The fact that dining in this warm, homey environment is also affordable means there really are real treasures in this magic kingdom.

le balzar

traditional brasserie

49 Rue des Écoles
Between Boulevard Saint-Michel and
Rue De La Sorbonne (5th Arr) *map E14*
Metro 10: Cluny la Sorbonne
33 (0) 1 43 54 13 67
www.brasseriebalzar.com

mon - sun 8p - midnight
dinner. full bar
$$ reservations recommended

Yes, Please: *kir royale, pommery royal brut,
poireaux vinaigrette, foie de veau poêlé, poulet rôti,
steak frites, gigot d'agneau fermier du quercy*

Here's a Parisian dining primer. Restaurants are generally formal, bistros are moderately priced neighborhood places with simple food. Brasseries offer even simpler fare like the "classics"—steak frites or roast chicken—and usually have an outside terrace, which can lead to some boisterous streetside dining. There are many quintessential Paris brasseries, each attracting a distinct clientele from streetwalkers to society types. **Le Balzar** is my favorite. Because it attracts an always-entertaining fashion-crowd, **Le Balzar** satisfies my eyes as much as my stomach.

les papilles

wine store with food worthy of a michelin star

30 Rue Gay-Lussac
Corner of Rue Saint-Jacques
(5th Arr) *map E15*
RER B: Luxembourg
33 (0) 1 43 25 20 79
www.lespapillesparis.com

mon - sat noon - 2p, 7:30 - 10p
lunch. dinner
$$ reservations recommended

Yes, Please: *08 domaine vacheron sancerre, eau de vie, lomo de thon, foie gras de canard à l'ancienne, le boudin blanc béarnais, assiette de jambon mr. arosagaray*

Remember in movies when the food would arrive under a gigantic silver cover? The unveiling of the dish always impressed me as elegance with a capital E. It's sad that these food domes seem to have fallen out of favor. At the stylishly homey bistro and wine cave **Les Papilles**, the food is served in the country equivalent—gorgeous tin-lined French copper pots. When my own personal copper pot arrived, the waiter removed the lid. As the gush of steam evaporated (my face felt dewy and renewed), it revealed a cauldron filled with bubbling, herb-infused meat and wine. I felt like I was a somebody.

6th / 45th

saint-germain-des-prés / montparnasse

eat

shop

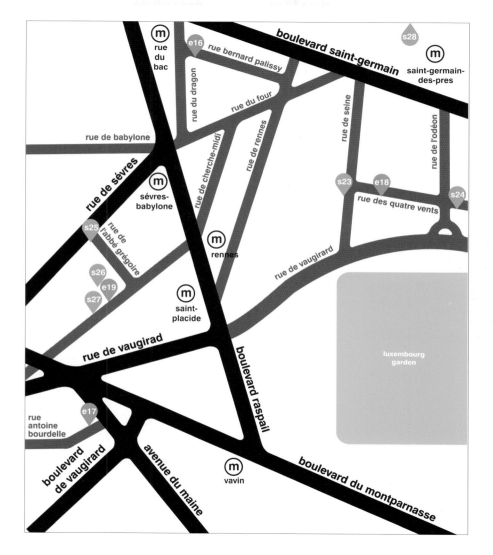

cire trudon

the oldest candle maker in france

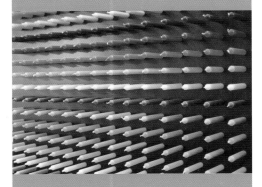

78 Rue de Seine
Between Rue Saint-Sulpice and
Rue Lobineau (6th Arr) *map S23*
Metro 4: Saint-Germain-des-Prés
33 (0) 1 43 26 46 50
www.ciretrudon.com

twitter @ciretrudon1643
mon - sat 10a - 7p

Yes, Please: *scented candles: carmalite, revolution, trianon, abd el kader, imperial pillar; candle busts: napoléon, marie antoinette; stink bombs, room sprays*

Cire Trudon was originally founded in 1643 and is the oldest manufacturer of candles in France. Within this long history, a highlight was supplying all of the candles to Versailles under Louis XVI. Though these candles were to provide light, I like to imagine ol' Louis sitting around in some silken, royal loungewear, listening to light jazz, with a **Trudon** candle pleasingly filling the room with scents of tuberose or vetiver. The shop has an amazing history, and today it offers candles of all shapes, scents and sizes. A perfect souvenir to take back to your own 10,000-acre country estate.

coco & co

all eggs, all the time

11 Rue Bernard Palissy
Between Rue de Rennes and
Rue du Sabot (6th Arr) *map E16*
Metro 4: Sait-Germain-des-Prés
33 (0) 1 45 44 02 52

mon – sat 10:30a – 5p
breakfast. lunch. treats
$-$$ first come, first served

Yes, Please: *orange presse, pastis, cocotte burger, brunch special, financier du jour, oeufs de saumon, tartinettes de villette canal, oeufs mayo*

A friend who cooked for years at a bed and breakfast told me: "You want breakfast, just put an egg on it." Meaning almost anything can be served at breakfast *avec un oeuf.* Coco & Co seems to have expanded on this idea. Everything at this tiny café comes with an egg, but not just in a breakfast type of way. The cocotte burger is a deliciously seasoned, fresh-cut patty served with a sunny side egg on top. The richness infused by the yolk makes the burger like a tartare and is ultra satisfying. Don't worry about the cholesterol—there is always *le Lipitor.*

kyrie eleison

modern clothing for women

15 Carrefour de l'Odéon
Corner of Rue Monsieur le Prince
(6th Arr) *map S24*
Metro 4: Odéon
33 (0) 1 46 34 26 91

tue - sat 10:30a - 7:30p
sun 2 - 6p

Yes, Please: *virginie castaway, cacharel, stella nova, le mont st. michel, erotokritos, yumi, ambali, gaspard yurkievich*

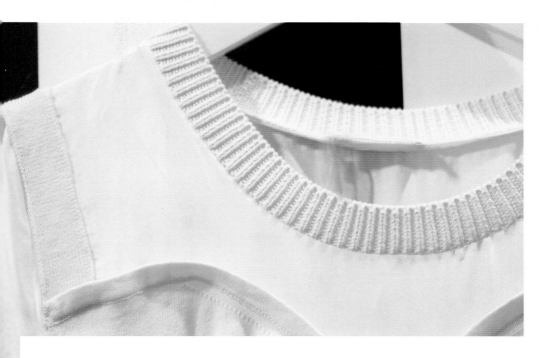

The other day I ran into an old college friend. It was great to see her until she noted my shirt and said, "It's funny, I remember that shirt from college." I realized with horror that the shirt had been worn through both the Clinton and the Bush administrations. I promptly burned it. If your closet is filled with clothes you danced to Cyndi Lauper in, perhaps you should visit **Kyrie Eleison**, where you can find clothing and accessories from emerging designers. You can't deny having lived through the Hammer Pants era, but with **Kyrie Eleison** you no longer have to wear them.

la cabane à huîtres

incredible oysters

4 Rue Antoine Bourdelle
Between Avenue du Maine and
Rue Falguière (15th Arr) *map E17*
Metro 4/6/12/13: Montparnasse
33 (0) 1 45 49 47 27

wed - sat 12:30 - 3p, 7 - 11p
lunch. dinner
$ cash only. reservations recommended

Yes, Please: *07 entre deux mers, 08 loupiac cérons,
huîtres moyennes, huîtres grosses, tranche foie gras, magret
de canard fumé, fromage pyrénées, canelé*

Here's the secret behind La Cabane à Huîtres. It's located a block from Gare Montparnasse, which serves France's Atlantic coast, and chef Francis has oyster beds near Bordeaux on that coast. So the oysters at **La Cabane**, which is no bigger than an American SUV, are ridiculously fresh. The 22 people that can wedge in here slurp the briny bivalves as fast as the cheerful Francis can shuck them, with everybody helping to pass *plateaus* across the room because it's too crowded for personal delivery. I helped myself to another glass of wine and marveled at what might be the perfect restaurant.

la crémerie

natural wine shop and small plates

9 Rue des Quatre Vents
Between Rue de Condé and
Rue de Seine (6th Arr) *map E18*
Metro 4: Odéon
33 (0) 1 43 54 99 30
www.lacremerie.fr

lunch fri - sat 1 - 2:30p
dinner tue - sat 5:30 - 10p
wine shop opens at 10:30a
lunch. dinner
$$ reservations recommended

Yes. Please: *07 philippe pacalet ruchottes-chambertin, champagne billecart-salmon, plateau de iberiques, paté de canard, boudin noir sur pan grillé*

Follow me here. Natural wines are different from organic wines in that they are produced without the aid of any commercial processes. Instead, they are harvested by hand and fermented with wild yeasts. This process produces interesting, esoteric wines usually from tiny producers. My wine-freak friends seek out these natural vinos like vampires on *Trueblood* tired of the synthetic stuff. Me? I just go to **La Crémerie**. Not only is their selection unsurpassed, the room is (surprise!) housed in a former crémerie, which is perfectly charming.

les yélos parisiens

cool bicycles and accessories

3 Rue de l'Abbé Grégoire
Between Rue de Sèvres and
Rue du Cherche-Midi (6th Arr) *map S25*
Metro 10: Vaneau
33 (0) 1 45 44 72 97
www.lesvelosparisiens.com

tue 10a - 1p, 2:30 - 7p wed 10a - 6p
thu - sat 10a - 1p, 2:30 - 7p
repairs / service

Yes, Please: *brompton folding bikes, yakkay helmets, brooks saddles, early rider wooden bikes, les vélos parisiens leather bags, nutcase helmets, sacoches de velo bags, kusua*

With the new Vélib system of rentable bikes throughout Paris, it couldn't be cooler to cycle. One problem, though, is that our stupid American credit cards, without smart chips, won't work in some of the machines. Hrmph. You can still rent a bike elsewhere in the city, but I highly suggest buying one at **Les Vélos Parisiens**, where they specialize in unusual bicycles. A pack of foldable bikes greets you as a reminder of how darn easy it would be to take one of these babies out of town for a country excursion—your own tour de France.

mamie
gâteaux
salon de thé

66 Rue du Cherche-Midi
Corner of Rue de l'Abbé Grégoire
(6th Arr) *map E19*
Metro 4: Saint-Placide
33 (0) 1 42 22 32 15
www.mamie-gateaux.com

tue - sat 11:30a - 6p
lunch. coffee / tea. treats
$-$$ cash only. first come, first served

Yes. Please: *thé mariage frères-bourbon, citron-miel, tarte tomates, aubergines, jambon cru, cake saumon fenouil, cake pruneaux lardons, crumble de legumes, tarte aux figues*

I used to think "ladies who lunch" had a rather glamorous occupation. I practically based my entire career on the idea of it. But seeing one too many St. John clad ladies air kissing and sipping on a lipstick-marked glass of chardonnay made me recoil. My fantasy and reality were way off. What I had in mind was more in the vein of **Mamie Gâteaux**. This tea salon exudes quiet chic. Delicate quiches and savory cakes served with a light salad are the perfect nosh for a social lunch. So wear something truly stylish here and leave the St. John at home.

mamie gâteaux brocante

antique shop owned by the mamie gâteaux people

68 Rue du Cherche-Midi
Between Rue de l'Abbé Grégoire and
Rue Jean Ferrandi (6th Arr) *map S26*
Metro 4: Saint-Placide
33 (0) 1 45 44 36 63
www.mamie-gateaux.com

tue - sat 11:30a - 6p
(if closed ask at the salon de thé)
cash only

Yes, Please: *antique camera obscura, vintage maps &*
posters, heavy french Linens, vintage cooking utensils, old
wooden toys, café au lait bowls, vintage french advertising

Don't get me wrong—I love a good Louis the XIV armoire, but I doubt I will ever be able to afford one. Nor is my house a baroque castle. Certain antiques seem to be for royalty or owners of software companies, but I prefer something a little more accessible that I can find at the *brocante* (antique market) run by the folks from **Mamie Gâteaux**. When two storefronts became available next to their salon de thé, they decided to sell the type of goods that decorate their restaurant—items ranging from cookware to French primary school maps and lesson books. Here's to the little people!

serendipity

furnishings for kids that make you happy

81 - 83 Rue du Cherche-Midi
Corner of Rue Jean Ferrandi
(6th Arr) *map S27*
Metro 4: Saint-Placide
33 (0) 1 40 46 01 15
www.serendipity.fr

tue - sat 11a - 7p

Yes. Please: *baladeuse lamp, wool balls, antique desk lamps, cool, industrial kids' beds, kid-sized adirondack chairs, wire wastebackets, felt birdhouse*

Life is full of times when you work hard to make something happen, like pursuing a coveted new job or working off some holiday pounds. Then there are times when an awesome gift falls out of nowhere: a snowstorm cancels your dental appointment or an incredible bistro opens a block from your house. These are serendipitous events and make life a little sweeter. **Serendipity**, the store, is filled with objects that make you happy in this way. Playful items for kids are not only beautifully designed but have a lighthearted take on childhood—and no luck is required to enjoy them.

talc
chic children's fashions

40 Rue Jacob
Between Rue Bonaparte and Rue de Seine
Metro 4: Sait-Germain-des-Prés
(6th Arr) *map S28*
33 (0) 1 42 77 52 63
www.talcboutique.com

mon 2 - 7p tue - sat 11a - 7p

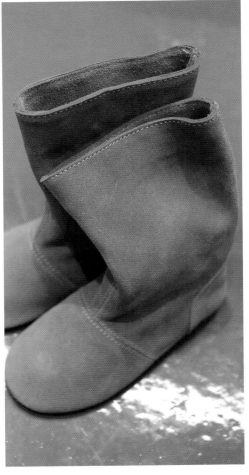

Yes, Please: *talc: robe louvre rivoli, sweat république,
burnou pull, short raspail, bilet luxembourg, blouse tuileries,
robe saint sulpice, rabbit hair/wool hat*

Why are the French so stylish? Because they have awesome kids' clothing stores. If you start cultivating the basics of style to a toddler, it's ingrained in them by the time they start dating. **Talc** starts kids early, offering clothes from three months and up, focusing on a cultivated but casual look. Think pea coats and printed cotton button-down shirts. These are mix-and-match classics, sophisticated yet carefree enough to give little Yves a look worthy of an art gallery opening by way of the playground. Well, that question is answered. Next up: Why does France have such delicious cheese?

7th / 16th arr.

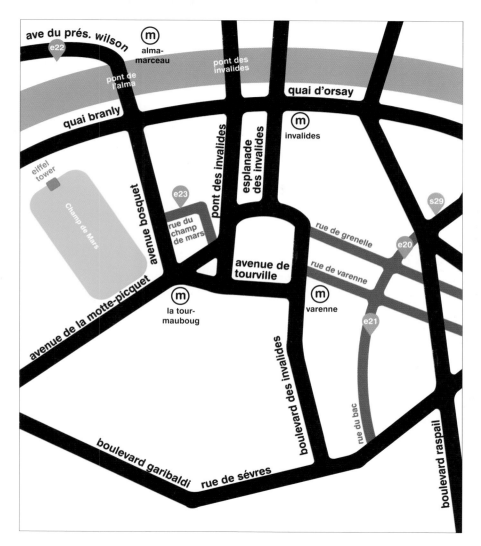

chapon
chocolatier
award winning chocolate

69 Rue du Bac, Near Rue de Grenelle
(6th Arr) *map E20*
Metro 12: Rue du Bac
See website for other locations
33 (0)1 42 22 95 98
www.chocolate-chapon.com

tue - sat 10a - 7:30p
treats
$-$$ first come, first served

Yes. Please: *mousses: équateur, sao tome,*
madagascar, cuba; praline with pink berries, lime ganache,
coulis de cassis

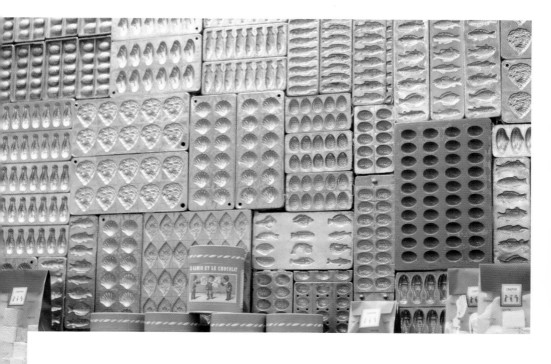

Just as I would rather not learn about my friends' sexual fantasies, I don't want to hear about their chocolate fantasies. They have them—I know, because I do, too. At least I do since I learned about the chocolate mousse bar at **Chapon Chocolatier**. Along with the ganaches and pralines is an honest-to-goodness, buy-it-by-the-kilo mousse bar where chocolate is whipped into heavenly suspension with differering intensities. This stuff is so good it makes me want to bring some home, put on my French maid outfit, and... I know, I know, t.m.i.

deyrolle

a paris institution, open once again!

46 Rue du Bac
Between Boulevard Saint-Germain and
Rue de l'Université (7th Arr) *map S29*
Metro 12: Rue du Bac
33 (0) 1 42 22 30 07
www.deyrolle.fr

mon 10a - 1p, 2 - 7p tue - sat 10a - 7p

Yes, Please: *framed & mounted exotic butterflies, french elementary school maps, taxidermied giraffe, seashells & coral, le prince jardinier candles*

Sometimes a terrible event happens and your friends think of you immediately. This happened recently when Bea Arthur died. My Facebook wall went crazy with condolences. Equally as grave was when a fire struck the mythical taxidermy world of **Deyrolle**. For years I have been proselytizing about this place's ability to command wonder from anyone lucky enough to visit its storied rooms. The day of the fire, dozens of friends reached out, stunned. I'm happy to report that **Deyrolle** has reopened and maintains the same glorious fascination it has always had. A phoenix rises.

la pâtisserie des rêves

dream pastries

93 Rue du Bac
Corner of Rue de Varenne
(6th Arr) *map E21*
Metro 12: Rue du Bac
33 (0)1 42 84 00 82
www.lapatisseriedesreves.com

tue - sat 9a - 8p sun 9a - 4p
treats
$-$$ first come, first served

Yes, Please: *le grand cru, le mille-feuille du dimanche, le moka, le st. honoré, le paris-brest, les éclaires, le tarte tatin, les viennoiseries*

La Pâtisserie des Rêves, the pastry shop of your dreams, is as advertised—the experience of buying something here is as fantastical as the treat itself. Famed pastry guru Philippe Conticini has staged the space like a Roald Dahl book. Buttery delicacies are displayed like rare and prized specimens under a network of glass cloches. To get a closer look, you simply ask for a cloche to be lifted, setting in motion pulleys and counterweights, all part of the elaborate Oompa Loompa type set-up. This might feel gimmicky if the confections weren't so exquisite. But don't worry Charlie, you need no golden ticket to enter.

marché avenue du président wilson

shopping for food as only the french can

Avenue du Président Wilson
Between Rue Debrousse and Place d'Iéna
(16th Arr) *map E22*
Metro 9: Alma Marceau or Iéna

wed and sat 7:30a - approximately 2:30p
outdoor market
$ - $$ cash only. first come, first served

Yes, Please: *coquille saint jacques, escargot, saint-nectaire fromage, moulé à la main demi-sel croquant butter, crêpes, pâté de campagne*

I don't care for the "trip of a lifetime" mentality where you have to visit all of the "must-see" spots on a claustrophobic tour bus. Yuck. The marvel of Paris comes from walking its streets. Crossing over the Pont Royal and realizing you are going through the massive, ornate gates of the Louvre is astounding every time. Similarly, shopping at one of the Parisian street food markets can provide drool-inducing memories. One of the toniest markets is the **Marché Avenue du Président Wilson**. Abundance is the theme here. I guarantee you'll enjoy this more than seeing dead old Napoleon in his tomb.

marie-anne cantin

a great cheese shop

12 Rue du Champ de Mars
Between Avenue Bosquet and
Rue Duvivier (7th Arr) *map E23*
Metro 8: École Militaire
33 (0) 1 45 50 43 94
www.cantin.fr

mon 2 - 7:30p tue - sat 8:30a - 7:30p
sun 8:30a - 1p
grocery
$-$$ first come, first served

Yes. Please: *fromage: saint marcellin sensation, bacaffe sèche, mucols, bleu de saqueville, tomme de savoie, fontainebleu maison, beurre cru*

I may never know the answer to this nagging question: Does food taste better in its native environment, or does the excitement about being in the place heighten one's senses? For example, if I were to magically transport one of **Marie-Anne Cantin**'s fabulous Roqueforts to my home in Portland, would it taste as phenomenal as when consumed in the shadow of the Eiffel Tower? Though Marie's stock of award-winning cheeses is among the best in Paris, would I feel the same about them stateside? Since my friends at U.S. Customs won't let me answer this question, it will remain a great mystery.

9th arr.

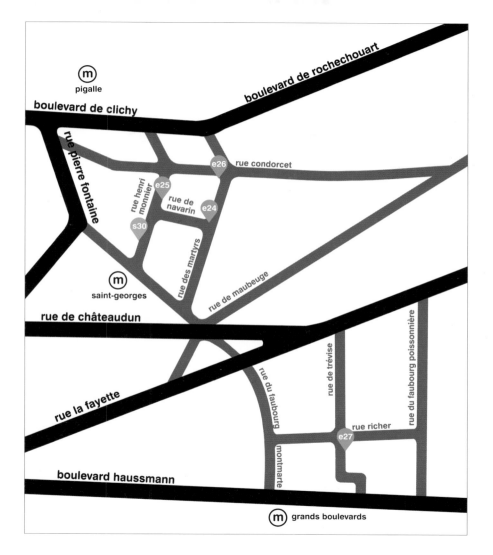

arnaud delmontel

all-around awesome bakery and pastries

39 Rue des Martyrs
Corner of Rue Navarin (9th Arr) *map E24*
Metro 12: Notre-Dame-de-Lorette
33 (0) 1 48 78 29 33
www.arnaud-delmontel.com

twitter @delmontel
wed - mon 7a - 8:30p
lunch. treats
\$ first come, first served

Yes, Please: *macarons, royal tart, tartelette citron, patte d'ours, campagne raisins, financiers, coeur frivole, millefeuille varié*

Naming your favorite baguette in Paris is like trying to name your favorite tree in the forest. Still people take a shot. At the top of many a list are the *bâtards* (loaves) at the famed *boulangerie* and *pâtisserie* **Arnaud Delmontel**. I can concur—these loaves are *la crème de la crème*. I used to live nearby and would often buy my bread here while picking up a few "extras": a flaky caramel and fleur de sel galette one day, a meringue and chocolate fantasy called *Le Vacherin* the next. I began to believe I must visit here daily because it was one-stop shopping. *Très* convenient.

chauvoncourt

a simple café

22 Rue Henri Monnier
Between Rue de Navarin and
Rue Victor Massé (9th Arr) *map E25*
Metro 12: Pigalle
33 (0) 1 48 78 26 03
www.chauvoncourt.com

mon - sat noon - 3p, 5:30 - 11p
lunch. dinner
$-$$ first come, first served

Yes, Please: *06 montepulciano d'abruzzo fonte venna, porchetta & salade verte, bresaola de boeuf, scamorza grillée & jambon de norcia, soufflé d'artichauts*

Every job has its cross to bear. Mine is having to eat in restaurants around the world. People often offer, "I'll be your assistant." But I know they couldn't handle the pressure. I am a highly trained eating athlete, having built my stamina over the years. Amateurs would crumble under the pressure of successive days of long lunches. Then again, there are times, like at **Chauvoncourt**, when dining is easy with Christophe Charton graciously hosting, delivering his charcuterie along with a whimsical story. OK, this doesn't sound tough, but sometimes it's a hard job. Honest.

cul de poule

another fun bistro

53 Rue des Martyrs
Corner of Rue Victor Massé
(18th Arr) *map E26*
Metro 2: Pigalle
33 (0) 1 53 16 13 07

mon - sat noon - 2:30p, 8 - 11p
lunch. dinner
$-$$ reservations recommended

Yes, Please: *06 gerard schueller pinot blanc, basque charcuterie, bavarois de petits pois, dorade rôtie sur peau & courgette, agneau épicé with aubergine confit*

Even though I'm a total francophile, sometimes French humor leaves me scratching my head. Jerry Lewis? Don't get it. But the comedy *Delicatessen*—about a butcher selling human meat—now that's entertainment! Along those lines (not the human meat ones, mind you) is **Cul de Poule**. Translation: Chicken Butt. This bistro is the talk of Paris, and it's as much about fun as it is about great food. Though handling ingredients sourced from top farmers and producers is no laughing matter and the food here is no joke, I've noticed everything tastes better when it's served with a wink and a smile.

pigalle
men's and women's fashions

7 Rue Henry Monnier
Between Rue Notre Dame and
Rue de Navarin (9th Arr) *map S30*
Metro 12: Pigalle
33 (0) 1 48 78 59 74
www.pigalleparis.com

tue - sat noon - 8p sun 2 - 8p

Yes, Please: *wood wood, dries van noten, phenomenon, ann demeulemeester, rick owens, sharon wauchob, gustavolins, manish arora*

When you look through the pages of French Vogue, it is easy to forget how hard it is to make the outfits look great. Mixing and matching clothes is easy if you are Grace Coddington, where lesser stylists just end up making a mess. At the new boutique **Pigalle**, the style within made me stand up and take notice. The mother and son team here mix haute and street, couture and sporty in a totally seamless, super chic way. So even if you aren't Rachel Zoe, no worries. The team at **Pigalle** has already done the hard work for you; just relax and buy.

supernature
super natural dining

12 Rue de Trévise
Between Rue de Montyon and
Rue Richer (9th Arr) *map E27*
Metro 8/9: Grands Boulevards
33 (0) 1 47 70 21 03
www.super-nature.fr

mon - fri noon - 2:30p, 7 - 10:30p
sat 7:30 - 11:30p sun 11:30a - 3:30p
lunch. dinner. brunch
$-$$ reservations recommended

Yes, Please: *jus d'orange fraîchement pressé, risotto potim-arron petits pois, tajine de poisson, cheeseburger aux jeunes pousses, oeuf cocotte bio au philadelphia cheese, carrot cake*

As I mentioned earlier in this book, healthy food in Paris is like the new bacon (veggie bacon perhaps?). Maybe this is too strong of a statement—but clean, healthy cuisine is certainly a breath of fresh air in this cheese-obsessed country. At **Supernature**, grains and sprouts are given their rightful recognition alongside lean proteins. In fact, coming to the popular Sunday brunch here is almost a throwback to the days of the old *Moosewood Cookbook*. I'm not complaining. I think healthy is the future. Even if this is simply a case of "what's old is new again," I've got my tie-dyed tank top ready to go.

10th arr.

canal / st. martin

eat

shop

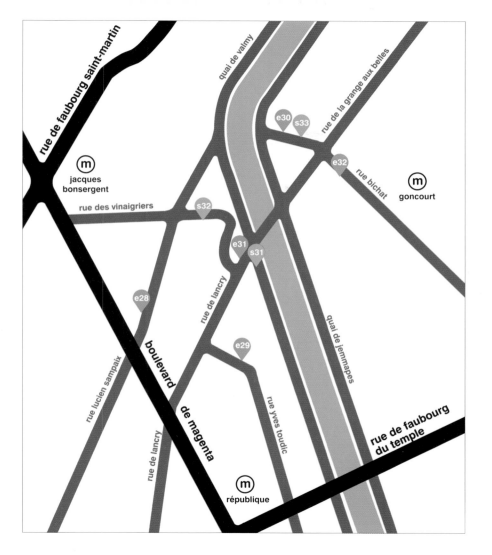

artazart

art and design bookstore

83 Quai de Valmy
Corner Rue de Lancry (10th Arr) *map S31*
Metro 5: Jacques Bonsergent
33 (0) 1 40 40 24 00
www.artazart.com

twitter @artazart
mon - fri 10:30a - 6:30p
online shopping

Yes, Please: *pinhole camera paint can, bensimon bags, lampe gras, "design & literature" by esther henwood, credit card stickers, lampe gras 206 chromée*

People often ask which neighborhood in Paris I would choose to live in. Honestly, a dart thrown at a map would produce a satisfactory answer—as long as Charles de Gaulle airport were out of play. Okay, I might secretly aim for the Canal St. Martin. This 'hood has great restaurants, interesting shops and a community of young creative types which makes it the middle of hipsterville. Also central, both geographically and in spirit, is **Artazart**—an art and design bookshop that opened when this area was still considered pioneering.

bob's juice bar

a shockingly healthy alternative

15 Rue Lucien Sampaix
Corner Boulevard de Magenta
(10th Arr) *map E28*
Metro 5: Jacques Bonsergent
33 (0) 9 50 06 36 18
www.bobsjuicebar.com

twitter @bobsjuicebar
juice bar: mon - fri 7:30a - 3p
kitchen: mon - sat 8a - 3p sat - sun 10a - 4p
breakfast, lunch
$ first come, first served

Yes, Please: *cocktail de jus, 100% fruit smoothie, housemade muesli, conscious chocolate, futomaki, tomato cashew nut soup & muffin, quinoa avocado salad*

You are never going to guess what the hottest trend in Paris is right now: health food! Made by an American!! *Mon Dieu*!!! Traditionally what has passed for "healthy" in Paris has been a salad weighed down with mounds of ham and Cantal cheese. Then **Bob's Juice Bar** opened on a side street off the Canal St. Martin, offering fresh-squeezed juices and vegetarian dishes. This is a business model that, until recently, sounded akin to opening an air conditioning shop in the arctic. It just goes to show, you can teach an old dog new tricks—as long as it's a veggie dog.

du pain et des idées

stellar bread and pastries in a stunning space

34 Rue Yves Toudic
Corner Rue de Marseille
(10th Arr) *map E 29*
Metro 5: Jacques Bonsargent
33 (0) 1 42 40 44 52
www.dupainetdesidées.com

mon - fri 6:45a - 8p
treats
$ first come, first served

Yes. Please: *pain des amis, escargot chocolat-pistache, mouna, tarte aux pommes, mini pavés, tarte aux peche, pain aux raisin, tarte citron*

Was it Mr. Atkins who made eating bread a guilt-ridden event? If so I want to punch him in the face. Or better yet, I would like to take him with me to the gorgeous **Du Pain et Des Idées** and make him sit, surrounded by the tremendous pastries. Then I would consume a chunk of the signature *pain des amis* inches from him, with its chewy texture balanced by a hearth-darkened crust. I'd eat it simply with salted butter, and never offer a crumb. Then I'd cut off another slice for myself and toss him a protein bar. Take that, Atkins.

la cantine de quentin

top-notch food for a bargain

52 Rue Bichat
Between Quai de Jemmapes and Rue de
la Grange aux Belles (10th Arr) *map E30*
Metro 4: Gare de l'Est
33 (0) 1 42 02 40 32

lunch tue - sun noon - 3:30p
store 10a - 7:30p
lunch. grocery
$-$$ reservations recommended

Yes, Please: *07 domaine les grands bois côtes du rhône, terrine de campagne maison, velouté d'artichauts, ravioles de royans, tartare de boeuf au couteau, cheesecake de johann*

Most people speak of our pallid economy as a negative. Always the optimist, I can think of an upside. As a response to the economic downturn, young, clever chefs are opening small neighborhood bistros with a focus on high-quality food but with economical prices. This is clearly illustrated at **La Cantine de Quentin**. Here you get top-shelf caliber but at the price tag of buck-night at your local sports bar. Daily lunch menus of hearty, deftly prepared dishes are served in a charming wine shop meets epicerie environment. And no drunk guys yelling at big-screen TVs. Score!

la galerie
végétale
art and flora

29 Rue des Vinaigriers
Between Quai de Valmy and
Rue Lucien Sampaix (10th Arr) *map S32*
Metro 5: Jacques Bonsargent
33 (0) 9 54 32 19 68
www.lagalerievegetale.com

tue - thu 10a - 2p, 3 - 7p
fri - sun 10a - 2p, 3 - 8p

Yes, Please: *succulents, cut flowers, orchids, rubber satchels, day of the dead masks, piñatas, recycled furniture, housemade candles*

When I shop with friends, they seem to resent my job. If we are in a store that doesn't quite pass muster, I will mention my favorite equivalent in another city. They think I'm jaded—I think I'm worldly. Regardless, it's impressive when I see a store doing something completely unique. Such is the case at **La Galerie Végétale**. Part flower shop, part art gallery, this warehouse space changes drastically and regularly, so each visit is a fresh and wonderful experience. Beware friends, I have something to name drop next time we're out and about.

le verre volé

natural wine shop and small plates

67 Rue de Lancry
Corner of Quai de Valmy
(10th Arr) *map E31*
Metro 5: Jacques Bonsergent
33 (0) 1 48 03 17 34
www.leverrevole.fr

mon - sun noon - 2:30p, 7:30 - 11p
lunch. dinner
$-$$ reservations recommended

Yes, Please: *07 oliver cousa, 06 morgon gamay noir;*
06 anjou aoc, la salade d'endive jambon cru, le boudin noir
confiture d'oignons, tartare de saumon "graveaux"

Wine sometimes costs less than a bottle of Perrier in France, so it's easy to make the leap that this might be a country of winos. It's the exact opposite. Really good wines at good prices seems to educate and cultivate the general public who seem more interested in quality than quantity. Which in turn supports places like **Le Verre Volé**. At this tiny cave, bottles from small, interesting producers line the walls. One can buy and fly, or order a bottle with a plate of the hearty fare for seven euros over the bottle price. This is a great way to try compelling vintages—and a far cry from the Three Buck Chuck experience.

pink flamingo pizza

pizza with attitude

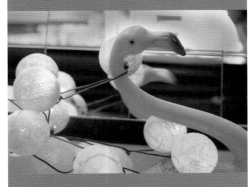

**67 Rue Bichat. Corner of
Rue de la Grange aux Belles
(10th Arr)** *map E32*
**Metro 5: Jacques Bonsergent
See website for other locations
33 (0) 1 42 02 31 70
www.pinkflamingopizza.com**

twitter @pflamingopiz
sun 1 - 11p mon 7 - 11:30p
tue - sat noon – 3p, 7 - 11:30p
lunch. dinner. wine / beer
$-$$ first come, first served

Yes. Please: *pelforth; pizzas; la bjork (smoked salmon,
egg & créme fraîche), l'aphrodite (eggplant, hummus &
pimento), l'almodovar (paella on pizza)*

How is it that a long-necked bird, exotic and pink, inspired everything from neon nightclub signs to large, gun-toting female impersonators? I will say that **Pink Flamingo Pizza** seems to have more in common with the latter, as it caters to a largely young, bohemian set. Pods of friends hang out along the banks of the canal with helium balloons used to identify their order. With the sometimes witty names and unusual combinations of ingredients, the pies have a sort of puckish attitude that one would expect from such a place. I'd say the bird is the word!

pop market

just for fun objects

50 Rue Bichat
Between Quai de Jemmapes and Rue de la
Grange aux Belles (10th Arr) *map S33*
Metro 5: Jacques Bonsergent
33 (0) 9 52 79 96 86
www.popmarket.fr

twitter @popmarkt
tue - sat 11a - 7:30p sun 3 - 7p

Yes, Please: *anne claire petit knit sack, ah, quel plaisir;*
mark's notebooks, baker backpack, birthday bunting,
tater pots, extratapete murals

One of my favorite mini-memories of working on this book took place at Pop Market. I was busy taking pictures when I saw two policemen walking in. Minutes later, I found myself near them as they were looking at models of American cop cars from the '50s. They found them incredibly hilarious and began to laugh. I chuckled too, laughing at them laughing. Then the train left the station as laughter built to a hilarious conclusion with tears running down our faces and one of them purchasing a model. No words were exchanged during this encounter. Names were changed to protect the innocent.

11th arr.

bastille

eat

shop

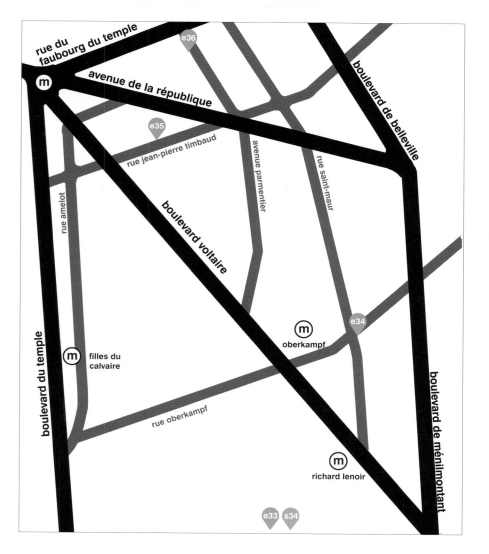

bistrot mélac

wine-focused bistro

42 Rue Léon Frot
Corner of Rue Emile Lepeu
(11th Arr) *map E33*
Metro 9: Charonne
33 (0) 1 43 70 59 27
www.mélac.fr

mon - sat noon - 2:30p, 7 - 10:30p
lunch. dinner
$-$$ reservations accepted

Yes. Please: *08 domaine laurens marcillac, 07 domaine ballorin et fils les chenevieres, pavé de boeuf avec pommes de terre, roti de veau braisé, plat du marché*

You never know what you are going to get when you spend an evening at the Bistrot Mélac. It all depends on who is sharing the room, or sometimes the table, with you. I have had joyous, convivial nights here with a soccer team celebrating the day's win, and cozy rainy nights when another bottle of wine sounded like the perfect antidote to the wet weather. Coming to **Bistro Mélac** is like life—sometimes it's raucous and other times not. The consistent part is your mustachioed host Jacques, who is always gracious, his wine key always at the ready.

la bague de kenza

maghrebi (north african) pastries

106 Rue Saint-Maur
Between Rue Oberkampf and Rue
Jean-Pierre Timbaud (11th Arr) *map E34*
Metro 3: Parmentier
See website for other locations
33 (0) 1 43 14 93 15
www.labaguedekenza.com

mon - sat 9a - 6p
treats
$ cash only. first come, first served

Yes. Please: *tea, rfissa, baklava, cravatte pistache,
dziriate, mhajeb, kesra, ghribia, cornet aux amandes*

The first time I ever tried sushi, I was more motivated by the way that it looked than dying to taste raw fish. In other words, I was attracted to the packaging and discovered I loved the contents. Sampling the Algerian pastries at **La Bague de Kenza** was similar. The mini watermelon-shaped pastries were gorgeous, so I was intent on eating one. All the pastries here are Maghrebi and are filled with honey and nuts as well as the essences of orange and rose waters. Everywhere you look, there are neatly arranged piles. Close your eyes, point a finger and whatever comes your way will be both pretty to look at and good to eat.

la pharmacie

a cheerful neighborhood bistro

22 Rue Jean-Pierre Timbaud
Corner Rue du Grand Prieuré
(11th Arr) *map E35*
Metro 3: Oberkampf
33 (0) 1 55 28 75 98
www.lapharmacie.net

mon - sun noon - 2:30p, 8p - midnight
lunch. dinner
\$\$ reservations recommended

Yes, Please: *08 cuvée des galets, 07 gimonnet-gonet brut,*
terrine à la moment, le burger normandaise avec foie gras,
faison rôti avec celeri & marrons, gnocchi & escargot

With a name like La Pharmacie you'd expect to feel good after eating at this charming restaurant housed in an old pharmacy. But what I discovered while eating here is that it wasn't just the delicious food that perked me up. **La Pharmacie** is like a happy pill and the whole neighborhood is taking the prescription. A birthday party was happening in one corner with friends lifting their glasses to the birthday boy. A couple sitting next to me struck up a conversation, giving me their hottest tips on the Paris restaurant scene. I left here totally sated. No need for Zoloft after.

le chateaubriand

sexy, creative cuisine

129 Avenue Parmentier
Between Rue du Faubourg du Temple and
Rue de la Fountaine au Roi
(11th Arr) *map E36*
Metro 11: Goncourt
33 (0) 1 43 57 45 95

tue – sat 8p – midnight
dinner
$$-$$$ reservations recommended

Yes. Please: *07 rené mosse anjou rouge, pommery champagne; encorrnets, carottes, bouguignonne; st pierre, cresson, liseron d'eau, cowbawa; poire crumble, mahaleb*

Recent articles have mentioned support groups developing for people depressed that they can't live in the iridescent fantasy world depicted in *Avatar*. Really? Get a fish tank! If you want to experience something truly sad, go to **Le Chateaubriand** and realize you won't be able to eat there every night. This fantasy world has chantilly colored walls washed in golden light—a perfect backdrop for the pack of fetching waiters who deliver the inventive food that is as surprising as it is comforting. **Le Chateaubriand** is spectacular. No 3D glasses required.

le jeune frères
hardware for the home

209 Rue du Faubourg Saint-Antoine
Between Rue Saint-Bernard and
Rue Faidherbe (11th Arr) *map S34*
Metro 8: Faidherbe-Chaligny
33 (0) 1 43 72 99 26
www.lejeunefreres.com

mon - fri 9a - noon, 2 - 6p
sat 9a - noon, 2 - 5p
online shopping

Yes. Please: *brass house numbers, cool cabinet pulls, casement window hardware, ornate keyholes, brass latches, lion door knockers, coat & hat hooks, door plaques*

Are there others like me? I ask myself this when I travel and obsess over all the utilitarian details I see. I'm positive no one else opens a café door over and over again, watching the way the latch snaps back by the simple action of a handsome spring. And I am sure that stopping in one's tracks to caress the latch of a Metro door, gauging the substantial and satisfying weight, is clearly certifiable. If others like me do exist, I suggest **Le Jeune Frères**, where you will get lost in the jumble of drawers that store everything from house numbers to light switches. It's a place with beautiful things for weirdos like me.

12th arr.

eat

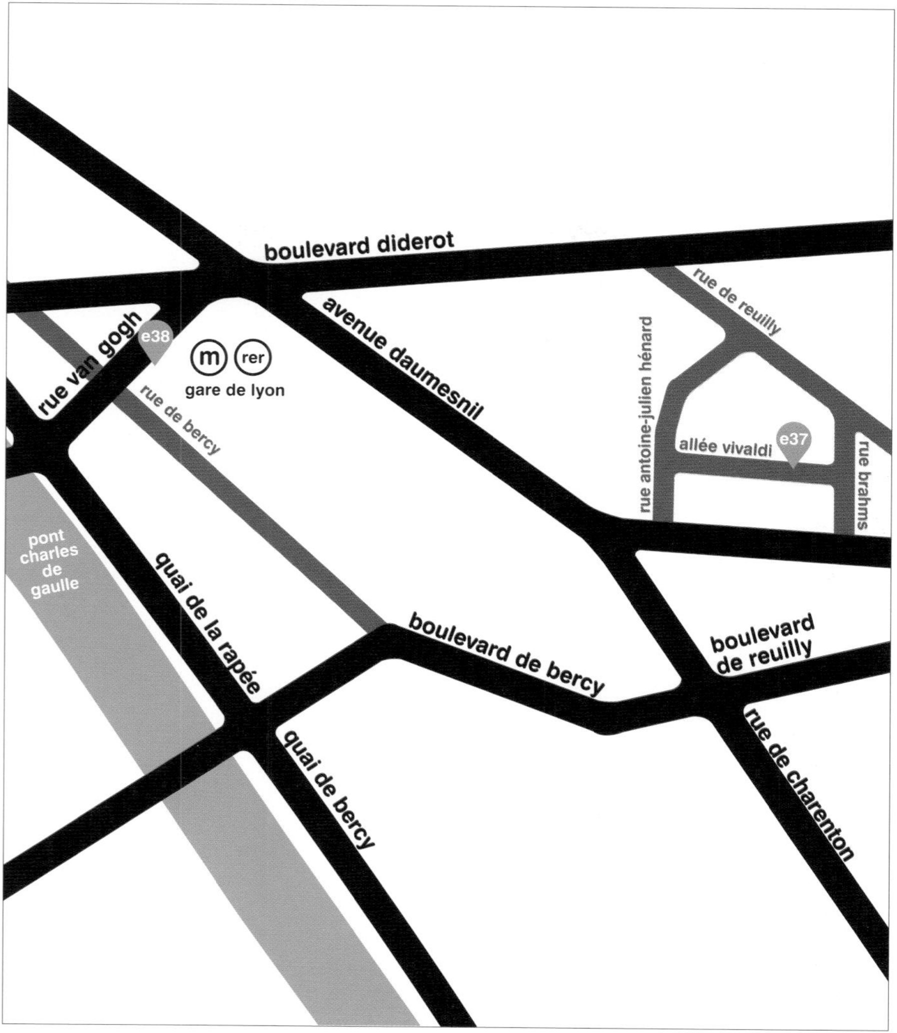

boulevard diderot
rue van gogh
e38
m
rer
gare de lyon
rue de bercy
avenue daumesnil
rue de reuilly
rue antoine-julien hénard
allée vivaldi
e37
rue brahms
pont
charles
de
gaulle
quai de la rapée
boulevard de bercy
boulevard
de reuilly
quai de bercy
rue de charenton

le janissaire

turkish cuisine with the trip

22 - 24 Allée Vivaldi
Between Rue de Reuilly and
Rue Hénard (12th Arr) *map E37*
Metro 8: Daumesnil
33 (0) 1 43 40 37 37
www.lejanissaire.fr

lunch mon - fri noon - 2:30p
dinner mon - sat 7 - 11:30p
$$ reservations accepted

Yes, Please: *buzbag turkish red wine, beignet de calamar, foie d'agneau poêle aux oignons assaisonne, onglet de boeuf grillé au gros sel, nois de saint jacques tava*

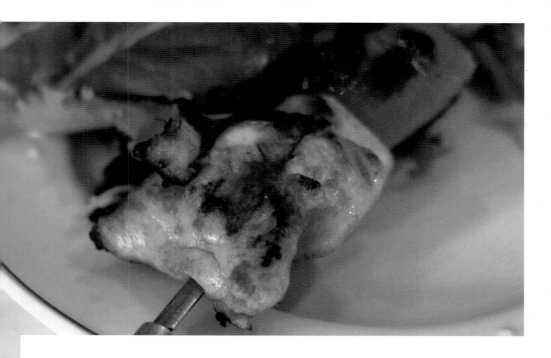

Most people who look forward to mangeing in Paris think primarily about the unpasteurized cheeses, delicacies in shells and buttery sauces. But this is nearsighted, as this is one of the most culturally diverse cities anywhere. A main destination of Turks and North Africans emigrating to Europe means killer kabobs and couscous are easily found. **Le Janissaire** is a fine example of where to get yummy meaty bites on a stick. Because it's located in the somewhat far-flung 12th Arr., you'd best think ahead before visiting here. But the tender grilled chunks of lamb are worth the trip—they're a Turkish delight.

le train bleu

like dining in le louvre

1Er Étage Gare de Lyon
Place Louis Armand (12th Arr) *map E38*
Metro 1: Gare de Lyon
33 (0) 1 43 43 09 06
www.le-train-bleu.com

mon - sat 11:30a - 3p, 7 - 11p
(bar open all day)
lunch. dinner. snacks. full bar
$$-$$$ first come, first served

Yes, Please: *"la lune bleue" ceylon tea, 06 alsace dopff &
irion gewurztraminer, isle flotant, brioche pain perdue avec
glace, poitrine de veau oubliée, escargot bourgogne*

Last year was an epic travel year for me. In a two-month span I was in six major cities in four countries. Seeing that many cities one after another illuminated their differences, with Paris being all about splendor and magnificence. An awe-inspiring example of this is **Le Train Bleu**, the belle époque restaurant in the Gare de Lyon. It is resplendent (so excited to finally be able to use this word). I rarely eat here as it's quite spendy—but for a cup of tea or a bottle of wine and some nibbles, it's a worthwhile expenditure, as this is a place of special beauty.

17th arr.

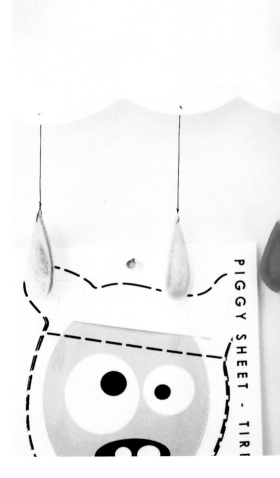

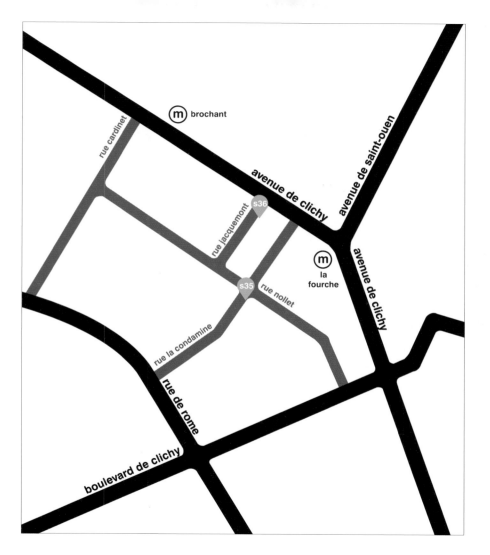

bda

fabulous vintage

46 Rue la Condamine
Corner of Rue Nollet (17th Arr) *map S35*
Metro 13: La Fourche
33 (0) 1 42 93 54 70
www.bastiendealmeida.com

tue - sat 11a - 8p
sewing classes

Yes, Please: *pedro rodriguez sequined number,
excentriques book, cabaret book, the house of nine, '80s geo-
metric sheath dress, goatskin coat, wigs done up in old styles*

The French do everything with a little more flair than we do. They do not send a dozen roses for a birthday, they send four dozen roses. Where our vintage stores often look like messy, moldering closets, Parisian vintage stores are incredible, like Bastien de Almeida's shop **BDA**. This place razzles and dazzles, with vintage gowns and dresses displayed in a club-like atmosphere. And though he's fond of a brand-name label, he cares more about what's beautiful, pointing to a gown displayed under a stuffed ostrich. An excellent example of where more is more.

french
touche

french-made objects

1 Rue Jacquemont
Corner of Avenue de Clichy
(17th Arr) *map S36*
Metro 13: La Fourche
33 (0) 1 42 63 31 36
www.frenchtouche.com

tue - fri 1 - 8p sat 11a - 8p
online shopping

Yes. Please: *voici, voila, voilou magazine; claire becquet-chaut jewelry, alpha beta, one bag one, estelle cusset cloches, marinettechou wire sculpture, les bons baisers booklets*

The act of making things and selling them is a core component to an economy. This remains true in Paris, where tiny shops exist doing work as simple as chair caning or leather bookbinding. It's reassuring to see this tradition continuing at **French Touche**. This eensy shop features works by talented artisans from around France, all partaking in the simple act of making something and selling it. From jewelry and handbags to mobiles and lighting, the range is wide and creative. What is consistent is the joy of knowing your purchase keeps the cogs turning in this artistic world.

18th arr.

montmartre

eat

e39 chéri bibi
e40 ets lion

shop

s37 marché aux puces de saint-ouen
s38 spree
s39 zut!

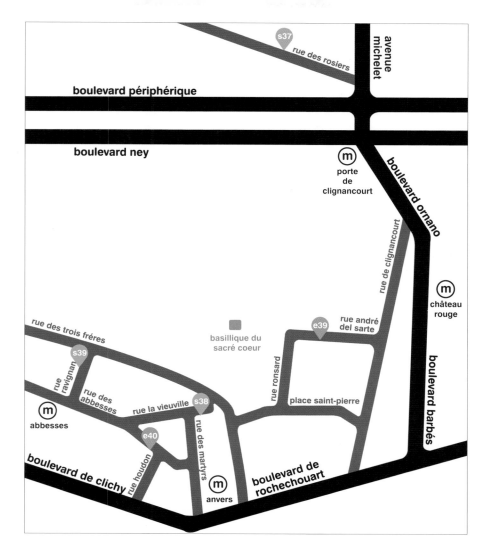

chéri bibi

fun bistro

45 Rue André del Sarte
Between Rue de Clignancourt and
Rue Charles Nodier (18th Arr) *map E39*
Metro 4: Chateau Rouge
33 (0) 1 42 54 88 96

mon - sat 8p - midnight
dinner. full bar
$$ reservations recommended

Yes, Please: *06 pascal lallement brut reserve, rhum arrangé, la terrine maison au porc & pruneaux, le fromage de tête de chez durard, le pavé de saumon mangues & sésame*

What's more important for a night out: delicious, innovative food or a super fun atmosphere? Depends on the night I'd say. There are times when studying each bite of your meal, like a scientist, is perfectly entertaining. Then there are nights when you want to feel like you've just been to Studio 54. Good news—**Chéri Bibi** will work for both kinds of moods. The menu has verve, with new takes on old classics made with confidence and panache. And I doubt the always-happening crowd would mind if you stood up and did a few Donna Summer moves after finishing your *plat du jour.*

ets lion

general store

7 Rue des Abbesses
Corner of Rue Houdon (18th Arr) *map E40*
Metro 12: Abbesses
33 (0) 46 06 64 71
www.epicerie-lion.fr

tue - sat 10:30a - 8p sun 11a - 7p
grocery. treats
$-$$ first come, first served

Yes, Please: *carumbes réglisse, le calisson, fruits confits, le monarque gateau, le petit nice thè, sirops de fruits confits, bougie candles, bulk huile d'olive*

A visit to the ultra-touristic Sacre Coeur is a must for any visitor to Paris—but don't let the performance of the mega-talented silver robot man miming to French pop music get in the way of the sweeping views. When you're done with the show, take a stroll to Rue des Abbesses. Surprisingly, the tourists will stay behind (for the next robot performance?) and you will find yourself in a charming neighborhood. Here lives **Ets Lion**, circa 1895, the de facto general store of the area. Browse the garden section and the fine foods and sample some candies knowing you are safe from robot man.

marché aux puces de saint-ouen

granddaddy of all paris flea markets

140 Rue des Rosiers
(18th Arr) *map S37*
Metro 4: Clingnancourt
33 (0) 1 40 12 32 58
www.parispuces.com/en

sat 9a - 6p sun 10a - 6p mon 11a - 5p

Yes, Please: *stalls within the market: biron, paul bert, serpette, cambo, dauphine, l'entrepôt, jules vallès*

This grandaddy of Paris flea markets is most commonly referred to by its metro stop: Clignancourt. You absolutely must visit here, but go with perseverance. Climbing the stairs out of the metro can feel like a sea of confusion. Follow the throngs past the vendors selling fake designer bags and rasta hats, and you will be rewarded. Hall after hall of diverse and astounding antiques provide mostly a window-shopping experience, unless you are in the market for a hotel-lobby-scaled chandelier. The splendor being peddled here is beyond your wildest dreams. But who knows? A special trinket may be within your grasp.

spree
the perfect store

16 Rue La Vieuville
Between Rue des Abbesses and
Rue des Trois Frères (18th Arr) *map S38*
Metro 12: Abbesses
33 (0) 1 42 23 41 40
www.spree.fr

mon 2 - 7p tue - sat 11a - 7:30p

Yes. Please: *isabel marant, marc by marc jacobs,*
il by saori komatsu, vanessa bruno bags, spree shoes, apc,
jo colombo lamp, great vintage furniture

In order for a business to be featured for a second time in this series (first eat.shop and now rather), they had to do something extraordinary, like open a killer new location, burn down and reopen with the same intangible magic as before, or be **Spree**. This place is *fantastique*, like two stores wrapped up in one: an inspired clothing store offering tightly curated young and stylish options, and an exceptional collection of vintage furniture, with offerings rivaling the best of mid-to-late century vintage furniture shops anywhere. **French Trotters**, **Deyrolle** and **Spree**: you're an elite group.

zut!

refurbished industrial antiques,
specifically clocks

9 Rue Ravignan
Between Rue des Trois Fréres and
Rue des Abbesses (18th Arr) *map S39*
Metro 12: Abbesses
33 (0) 1 42 59 69 68
www.antiquites-industrielles.com

wed - sat 11a - 1p, 4 - 7p or by appointment
cash only. online shopping

Yes, Please: *railway enameled ato clocks, double faced le-*
paute clocks, '40s singer stool, jean prouvé work chair, gras
de marbrier lamp, eight foot tall welded eiffel tower

A pox upon you, Atlantic Ocean! Because of your hugeness, I am unable to carry home many things I desperately desire. For example, If **Zut!** were in Kansas City, I would have no reservations buying one of their amazing refurbished train station clocks and driving it home. But the silly ocean makes that plan impossible. I guess I could buy a boat, learn to drive it and bring the clock home via the Panama Canal. It would be worth it to have some of these cool vintage items. I guess, though, I'll accept reality and fly home with more modest souvenirs tucked in my carry-on bag as I curse the big blue Atlantic below.

20th arr.

belleville

eat

e41 le baratin

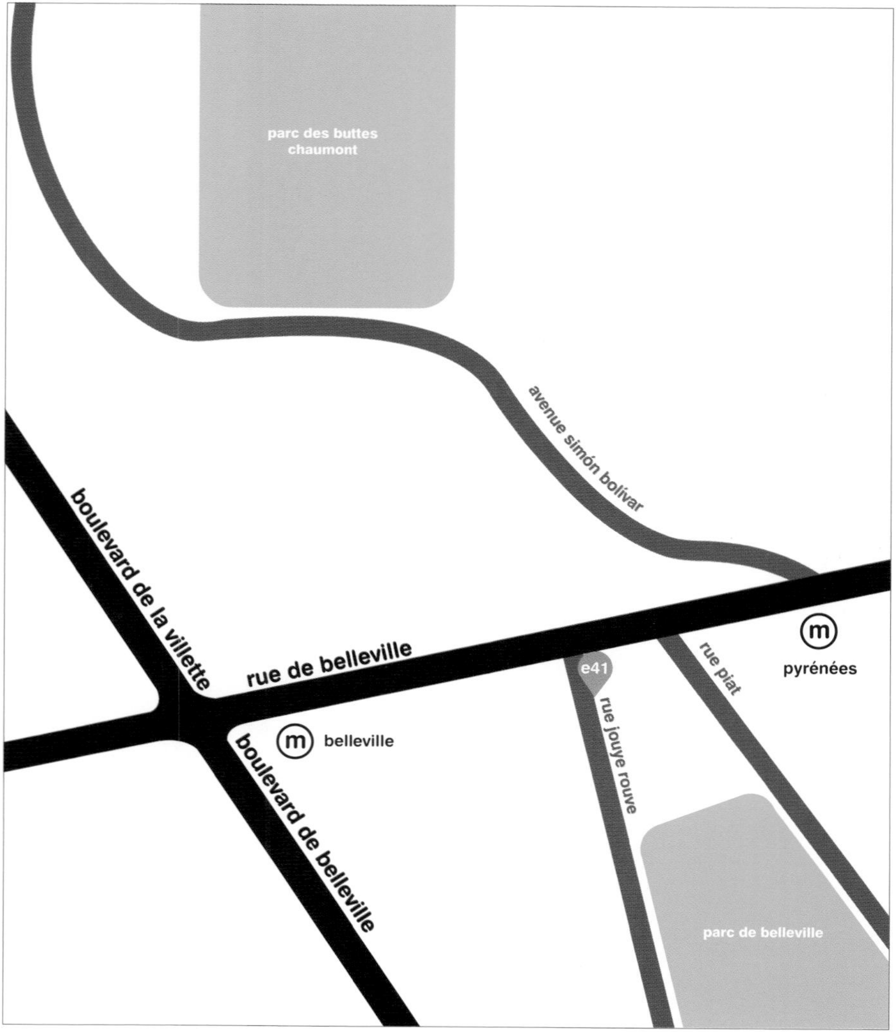
parc des buttes chaumont
avenue simón bolívar
boulevard de la villette
rue de belleville
e41
rue piat
pyrénées
m
rue jouye rouve
m
belleville
boulevard de belleville
parc de belleville

le baratin

incredible food influenced by france, italy and argentina

3 Rue Jouye Rouve
Between Rue de Belleville and
Rue Lesage (20th Arr) *map E41*
Metro 11: Pyrénées
33 (0) 1 43 49 39 70

tue - fri noon - 2:30p, 8 - 11p sat 8 - 11p
lunch. dinner
$$ reservations recommended

Yes, Please: *07 bourgogne hautes côtes de beaune, muscat de patras, tarte de blettes & parmesan, boullon de cabillaud et tomates, colinot frit, crème de noisette*

Once in a while I taste food so good, I realize I am in the presence of someone with "the touch." Raquel Carena, the chef at **Le Baratin**, has "it." When I took a bite of the *colinot frit*, I instantly got "the feeling," and across my face was plastered "the look." To have "the touch" is a special talent where a chef makes food that tastes like no one else's—everything is just a little more: flavorful, delicate, nuanced. I don't think you can learn "the touch;" you must be born with it. I don't have "it," that's to be sure—so I'll just eat the food of those that do have "it" and be supremely happy.

finito

happy travels to you

rather *paris*

isbn-13 9780984425365

copyright 2011 ©swiftrank. printed in the usa

editing / fact checking + production: chloe fields
in design master: nicole conant
map design + production: julia dickey + bryan wolf

thx to our friends at designers & agents for their hospitality and their support of the rather experience. please visit > designersandagents.com

rather is distributed by
independent publishers group > www.ipgbook.com

to peer further into the world of **rather** and to buy books, please visit **rather.com** to learn more